Tulips and Maple Leaves in 2010

Perspectives on 65 years of Dutch-Canadian Relations

Tulips and Maple Leaves in 2010

Perspectives on 65 years of Dutch-Canadian Relations

Edited by

Conny Steenman Marcusse
&
Christl Verduyn

Barkhuis
Groningen 2010

Book cover design, book interior design and typesetting: Nynke Tiekstra ColtsfootMedia – Noordwolde

ISBN 9789077922699

Contents

M

Het Loo, March 2010

Dear Canadians and Friends of Canada,

This May 2010, on the occasion of the 65th anniversary of the liberation of the Netherlands by Canadian troops in the Allied Forces in 1944 and 1945, many events will take place in commemoration and celebration, both in the Netherlands as in Canada. My husband and I feel honoured to be present at several of these celebrations also this anniversary year, as we want to underline the importance of remembrance and paying tribute to our liberators.

I am delighted with the contribution to these events by this book of historical and contemporary photographs, interviews with Dutch and Canadian citizens, and essays by students and young graduates on topics, reflecting on the past and looking ahead to the future.

During World War II, Canada extended a warm welcome to my family and me, offering us a home in Ottawa while our country was in the grip of the occupying forces. The role of Canada as liberator of our country has built the foundation for many years of friendship and cooperation between our countries and citizens.
It gives me great pleasure to see our good relations developing into the future, with activities and projects such as this book. My warmest congratulations to its editors and contributors.

Margriet.

Courtesy Anke Teunissen

The Hague, Colloquium for the essayists and their instructors sponsored by Dutch Foreign Affairs on 3 March 2010.

Acknowledgements

The preparation and production of a book is a collegial and collective effort, requiring not only the work of writers and editors, but also the efforts of copyeditors, book designers, and publishers, as well as the support of numerous organizations. We are honoured and privileged to acknowledge and thank all who have participated in this timely and important book.

The idea for this project unfolded through many stages and concepts. However, it only became reality in mid-January 2010, when crucial financial support was confirmed by the Western Hemisphere Department of *Het Ministerie van Buitenlandse Zaken* [the Dutch Ministry of Foreign Affairs] in The Hague. This decision was the culmination of a series of interesting and productive conversations at the Ministry, and with interested parties, about how best to mark the 65th anniversary of the liberation of the Netherlands by Canadian troops at the end of the Second World War. Many possibilities were considered, including a national conference, local commemorations, and the publication of a book of photographs depicting that historical moment in history. Dr. Conny Steenman Marcusse, President of the Association for Canadian Studies in the Netherlands (ACSN), suggested that the new generation – students and young people – could be brought into the project through the contribution of short essays for the volume. A further novel idea came out of these conversations: to include interviews with both Dutch and Canadian citizens on the general topic of Dutch-Canadian relations and the Second World War. Thus, this project involved an array of ideas, initiatives, and objectives, and ultimately concluded with the collection of photographs, interviews, and essays that is presented here.

With the financial support of Dutch Foreign Affairs in place, the book was developed under the co-editorship of ACSN president Dr. Conny Steenman Marcusse and, from Canada, Dr. Christl Verduyn, Professor of Canadian Studies and English Literature at Mount Allison University, Sackville, New Brunswick. Colleagues on a previous, related project – the Dutch World War II "underground photographer" Emmy Andriesse – their collaboration on this book was again a rewarding and productive one, which benefited enormously from the generous participation of its many contributors: the interviewees, and their interviewer, translator, and photographer, as well as the essayists and their instructors. The helpful staff at Dutch Foreign Affairs, the supportive members of the ACSN Board, as well as the director and the designer at Barkhuis Publishing also deserve our appreciation and praise. Special thanks and gratitude are extended to the photographers, both unknown and known, who captured and preserved history, as it was happening, for the world and for the future. The importance of their contribution grows with each new generation. Allow us to say a few more words about the many individuals and the organizations that supported this book.

In the early conversations with Dutch Foreign Affairs about a project to celebrate the 65th anniversary of the liberation, a number of individuals offered particular attention and encouragement. Deputy Director Peter Potman initiated the project and Advisor Dirk Knook coordinated the preparatory activities. Their interest in and support of the project were critical and greatly appreciated, as was the colloquium for the essayists and their instructors sponsored by Dutch Foreign Affairs on 3 March 2010.

The project enjoyed the further support of the ACSN (Association for Canadian Studies in the Netherlands) Board, and takes its place alongside many previous important contributions to Dutch-Canadian relations produced by the Association and its members. Created in 1985, under the auspices of the Canadian Department of Foreign Affairs and International Trade, the Association for Canadian Studies in the Netherlands has published thirteen volumes in the series "Canada Cahiers", including *Building Liberty: Canada and World Peace, 1945-2005*, edited by Conny Steenman Marcusse and Canadian writer Aritha van Herk. Past and present ACSN Board members have contributed to the accomplishments of the Association and its publications as well. Dr. Cornelius Remie co-founded the Association (with Professor Ben Hoetjes and the late Professor August Fry) and is its past president. Dr. Remie initiated the first all-European Canadian Studies conference in 1990 in The Hague, and founded the European Network for Canadian Studies. He also served as president of the International Council for Canadian Studies (2007-2009). He has made numerous and major contributions to the study of Canada in the Netherlands and in Europe, and he has received the Meritorious Service Medal. Professor Dr. Jaap Lintvelt held the first Chair in Canadian Studies in the Netherlands until his retirement from the Department of Romance Languages and Cultures at the University of Groningen. The University of Groningen is home to the country's only Centre for Canadian Studies, currently under the directorship of Dr. Jeanette den Toonder. At Radboud University in Nijmegen, Professor Dr. Hans Bak, a long-time ACSN Board member and one of the Association's past presidents, teaches Canadian literature to students at the Master's level. Members of the Association for Canadian Studies in the Netherlands have clearly been active and productive contributors to Dutch-Canadian relations. In this latest project, ACSN treasurer Fred Toppen, who teaches at the University of Utrecht, is owed a special note of thanks for his invaluable assistance with budgetary details.

This volume would not have been possible unless a number of individuals had agreed to be interviewed and to generously share their thoughts and experiences. We would like to thank Dr. Pieter Beelaerts van Blokland, Jan Piëst, Eke Foreman-van der Woude, Mary Derr-de Jong, Kristen den Hartog, Malcolm Campbell-Verduyn, André Gingras, Sandra van Rijn, Bob Hofman, and Lia and Helena Dell'Orletta. It took effort and imagination to consider whom to interview and which ideas and areas to include. For their role in this important part of the project, we would like to thank Lisa Lavoie, Marcel Louwman, and Melanie ter Meulen at the Canadian Embassy in The Hague; Albert Hartkamp, secretary of the national committee "Thank you Canada & Allied Forces"; Jan Boers and Wolfgang Oude Aost of the organization "Liberation Children"; and Mary Erskine, Senior Educational Tour Manager of EF Tours. Journalist Olga van Ditzhuijzen conducted the interviews and generated responses and reflections in a lively and unique fashion. Photographer Anke Teunissen successfully captured the different personalities of the individuals interviewed in the Netherlands. We wish to thank them for their terrific work.

We are pleased to acknowledge and thank the young essayists, and the instructors who supervised their work. Three institutions and their members supported this enterprise: at the Roosevelt Academy in Middelburg, Dr. Giles Scott-Smith, working with Moritz Baumgaertel, Jacqueline Breidlid, Jesse Coleman, Djeyhoun Ostowar, and Arlinda Rrustemi; at Radboud University, Nijmegen, Professor Dr. Hans Bak, working with Hans van Riet, Irene Salverda, and Ruben Vroegop; and at the University of Groningen, Dr. Jeanette den Toonder of the Centre for Canadian Studies, and her students Emma Kutka and Marijn van Vliet.

Choosing the photographs for this volume was a labour of love and admiration. We wish to extend heartfelt posthumous thanks to the photographers who have passed away, and warm appreciation to the contemporary photographers who agreed to share their work. We would also like to express our gratitude to the many individuals who assisted with obtaining permissions and other professional and technical details related to the photographs: Flip Bool and Carolien Provaas, *Nederlands Fotomuseum*, Rotterdam; Gert Jan van 't Holt, Canadian War Cemetery, Holten; David Barnouw and Harco Gijsbers, Netherlands Institute for War Documentation (NIOD), Amsterdam; and Marieke Monsieurs, *Koninklijke Bibliotheek* [National Library], The Hague.

This was a particularly time-sensitive book project, conceived, produced, and published in a very concentrated period of time to a strict and unforgiving deadline. The successful appearance of this volume would not have been possible without the prompt turnaround on translations by Mark Baker of Wordsmiths: Writing, Editing, Translation, the proofreading assistance of Lynn van der Velden-Elliott and Rowan Hewison, and most especially the expertise of Nynke Tiekstra and Roelf Barkhuis, respectively book designer and director of Barkhuis Publishing. Working with them was a pleasure and a delight. We wish also to acknowledge the support and understanding of our families and friends as we completed this project, particularly during the final, feverish lead-up to publication deadline when we went into "editorial retreat". To them – and to all who were involved in this project – our most sincere thanks and appreciation.

Introduction

Perspectives on 65 years of Dutch-Canadian Relations

Conny Steenman Marcusse and Christl Verduyn

This volume celebrates three important and interconnected moments and themes in the rich and rewarding history of Dutch-Canadian relations. The first is the liberation of the German-occupied Netherlands by Canadian troops in the fall of 1944 and the spring of 1945. May 2010 marks the 65th anniversary of this historic event. The second is the significant and consequential post-war emigration to Canada of countless Dutch families and individuals, many of whom remained in Canada and some of whom returned to the Netherlands. The third component of this project is the contemporary collective desire – in both the Netherlands and in Canada – to ensure that the importance, understanding, and memory of these past events extend into the future.

A substantial and imaginative example of this third component is the May 2010 trip to the Netherlands of nearly 2,000 Canadian students to visit the graves of the Canadian soldiers whose lives were lost in the liberation of the Dutch. A crucial objective of this volume is that it return to Canada with each and every one of these 2,000 students, as well as with visitors and war veterans, to share its images and stories with their friends and families. This book will thus contribute meaningfully to the consolidation and extension of the knowledge and understanding of the formidable connections between Canada and the Netherlands.

This introduction will present a brief overview of the volume and its sections and main themes. From the outset, photographs were to be a key component of the book; indeed, they take pride of place and, together with some graphics, set the stage in Part I of the volume. The photographs are presented in a broadly chronological order – in three parts or movements. First are striking images of the liberation in 1944 and 1945. These are followed by photographs that capture the extents and elements of Dutch emigration to Canada. Part I concludes with contemporary photographs that reflect the present – as recently as the 2010

Conny Steenman Marcusse

Olympics in Vancouver, Canada, where, on more than one occasion, Canadian and Dutch athletes shared the medal podium, and where the Dutch State Secretary of *Volksgezondheid, Welzijn en Sport* [Public Health, Welfare, and Sport], Jet Bussemaker, addressed veterans on 18 February 2010.

The photographs in Part I articulate and frame the themes pursued in Parts II and III of the volume, in particular the experiences of liberation, emigration, and memory, as well as various athletic, artistic, cultural, and academic achievements. In many ways, the latter themes recognize both the positive and the painful aspects of the former themes. It is true that memories of liberation are often reported in celebratory tones. And emigration may generally be seen to have led to eventual success and happiness. But the experiences of liberation and emigration were also often difficult, challenging, and painful. Loved ones were lost on the battlefields or to starvation during the Hunger Winter of 1945. Families were separated by a vast ocean, and financial resources were often insufficient to make visits possible. These experiences form part of the collective and individual memories of the Canadian liberation of Holland and the emigration of many from the Netherlands to Canada. The photographs, interviews, and essays collected here do not avoid these less celebratory moments, although they may feature less prominently. This reflects in part our understanding of and respect for the feelings and privacy of those who personally – and often painfully – experienced the difficulties of war and emigration.

In Part II, we present ten personal interviews with Dutch and Canadian individuals. These were chosen from a list of dozens of potential candidates. Space considerations required us to focus on a limited number, reflecting as wide an array of walks of life and experience as time and circumstances would allow. In the last analysis, interviews were conducted to reflect the key components and aims of the volume. In these interviews, readers will meet the president of "Thank you Canada & Allied Forces", the Dutch national committee that welcomes veterans; an eyewitness to the liberation of the Dutch city of Groningen; a war bride; a liberation baby; a Canadian writer on the subject of her Dutch heritage; a grandson of Dutch immigrants; the Canadian director of Rotterdam Dance Works; a Canadian maple syrup entrepreneur living in Leiden; the director of the project "Echoes", which links Canadian veterans with Dutch students; and finally, a Canadian mother and her teenage daughter on a visit to the Netherlands for the 65th anniversary of the liberation. Their conversations with journalist and interviewer Olga van Ditzhuijzen are as wide-ranging and engaging as they are informative and moving. These interviews connect the past to the present, and open possibilities to the future.

Christl Verduyn

As previously noted, this volume contemplates the strengthening and deepening of ongoing Dutch-Canadian relations as well as their appreciation and understanding. To this end, the interviews in Part II include information about plans and initiatives for future events. In some instances, these will replace efforts that have sustained connections between the two countries for many years. These efforts have successfully accomplished their mission and it is time to consider new initiatives to address fresh challenges and opportunities in the future. Thus, for the organization "Thank you Canada & Allied Forces," May 2010 marks the last time that events will be organized on a national scale. The plan for the future is to establish more locally-based events that will pay tribute to the men and women who fought for freedom and peace. A number of new sites of commemoration and celebration have already opened. For example, the Liberation Museum Zeeland was officially inaugurated in October 2009. H.R.H. Princess Margriet of the Netherlands performed the honours. She was born in Ottawa during the war, when the Dutch Royal family were compelled to leave the Netherlands and chose Canada for its refuge. One of the most frequently recounted moments in the collective war memory of the Dutch and Canadians is the Canadian government's gesture to declare the Princess's birth room in Ottawa to be part of Dutch territory. This allowed the Princess to be born a Dutch citizen. Princess Margriet and her husband Professor Mr. Pieter van Vollenhoven have played a substantial and prominent role in the evolution and development of Dutch-Canadian relations and events over the past 65 years, including the inauguration of the Canadian War Museum in Ottawa in 2005. Every spring, countless Canadians enjoy the bounty of tulip gardens that beautify their nation's capital, thanks to the thousands and thousands of bulbs that are sent annually by the Netherlands in appreciation of Canada's wartime hospitality to the Dutch Royal family and Canadians' contribution to the war.

Part III features essays that were written by current students and recent graduates from three Dutch post-secondary institutions: the Roosevelt Academy, Middelburg, in the south of the country; Radboud University, Nijmegen, in the east; and in the north, the University of Groningen. The young essayists undertook to address one of the priority issues identified by the Canadian Department of Foreign Affairs and International Trade (DFAIT) in its 2008 document, "Understanding Canada", including peace and security, economic development and prosperity, democracy and human rights, management of diversity, and the environment. With the assistance and guidance of their instructors, Dr. Giles Scott-Smith (Roosevelt Academy, Middelburg), Professor Dr. Hans Bak (Radboud University, Nijmegen), and Dr. Jeanette den Toonder (Centre for Canadian Studies, University of

Groningen), the essayists tackled a number of these challenging topics – while facing the same constraints of publication time and space as the other sections of the book. These essays provide a remarkable cross-national Dutch-Canadian "snapshot" of the next generation's reflection on some of the most compelling issues confronting them and their children. They are thoughtful and serious on the subject of Afghanistan, the threat of climate change, the challenges of cultural difference, and the debates over human rights. They are also personal, sharing moments of joy and insight: cycling the streets of Vancouver; driving the Dempster Highway in Canada's North; skating the Ottawa canal in winter; visiting the Canadian military base in Gagetown, New Brunswick; and getting to know Canada from coast to coast.

Complementing the Dutch students' involvement in this volume, Canadian students are also directly involved in the celebration of the 65th anniversary of liberation. In May 2010, 2,000 young Canadians will visit the Canadian war cemeteries in Groesbeek, Holten, and Bergen op Zoom, for an extraordinary, emotional, and educational experience that is sure to become a lifetime memory. Of the more than 6,000 Canadian soldiers who are buried in the Netherlands, 5,128 rest in these three cemeteries, which are located nearest the sites of some of the final, critical battles of the Second World War during the fall of 1944 and the spring of 1945. The southern regions of the Netherlands were liberated before the northern parts of the country, including the capital city of Amsterdam, which remained occupied and deprived of food supplies throughout the bitter winter of 1945, known as the Hunger Winter. By the time the German army surrendered to the Allied Forces on 5 May 1945, the majority of Dutch cities had been liberated by Canadians and the Allied Forces.

Canadian troops were instrumental in helping a war-ravaged country get back on its feet. That there were some stumbles along the way was probably inevitable, and this experience is one of the subjects of *Oranje bitter, Nederland bevrijd!* ["Bitter orange, the Netherlands freed"], a joint exhibition of the National Library and the National Archives in The Hague, 28 April – 4 July 2010. Among the exhibition's features is a series of postcards that depict, in amusing and suggestive ways, the relations between Canadians and Dutch citizens during and after liberation. Samples of these postcards are included in Part I of this volume. Whatever the stumbles that could and did occur, the Dutch welcomed their liberators in 1944 and 1945. Flags were draped everywhere. The population decked itself in dashes of orange in a collective expression of celebration and appreciation that has become a tradition ever since, and is the impetus behind the events planned for 2010 and beyond. A Canadian War Cemetery Information Centre in Holten, for example, is being developed, which will digitize all materials from the Second World War and build a data base about the Canadians killed in action.

It is gratifying and exciting to see that the passage of time – 65 years! – has dulled neither our historical imagination nor the intensity associated with the events of wartime liberation and post-war emigration and settlement. These contemporary institutional and program initiatives build on 65 years of events and commemoration, and lay new and exciting foundations for future interactions and connections between Dutch and Canadians. It is in this spirit and context that this volume is presented. It provides images, records, words, reflections, and aspirations from both the past and the present. Its readers are encouraged to explore and enjoy its diversity, and to ensure that its messages and objectives find their place in the future.

April 2010

Photo/ Graphics

55 Socks
A poem by MARIA JACOBS

That last winter of war had its compensations
We had no food except turnips and tulip bulbs.
But we did have a white bedspread.

Barter was now the only thing, but who would want
a bridal bedspread when even the most essential clothing
could not be had for love nor money.
Who had love to spare anyway – survival was all.

The four of us, female, two Jews, one gentile
and one ignorant child attacked the bedspread
early one morning it the room at the back.
In six days we knitted from its crinkled unravellings
Fifty-five socks. That finished the cotton.

The socks folded neatly in pairs, the mate less one
In her pocket, my mother set out on a tireless bike
to trade with the farmers. None wanted socks
but finally at dusk one well-fed woman warmly dressed,
arms akimbo, was ready for business.

A side of bacon, two dozen eggs, five pounds of wheat
and a scruffy chicken bought her the socks.
Then my mother remembered the lonely extra
and would throw it in for a quart of milk
if the farmer's wife wanted.

Oh yes, she confessed, in a whispering voice,
she wanted. She did not need socks, but she planned
to unpick them, for she loved to knit and her heart
was set on a lacy white bedspread.

From A *Safe House: Holland 1940-1945*
(Woodstock, Ontario: Seraphim Editions, 2005)

A still from the animation film "55 Socks". Dutch-Canadian filmmaker, Co Hoedeman, in co-production with the Dutch company, Coconino, is making this film based on Dutch-Canadian writer Maria Jacob's poem, "55 socks", which describes the sacrifices and ingenuity of those who survived the Hunger Winter of 1944-45 in the Netherlands.

An Allied Forces tank rolls by a signpost for the Dutch towns of Goes, Vlissingen, and Bergen op Zoom in the south of the Netherlands, which was liberated in the fall of 1944. The north was liberated in the spring of 1945.

Courtesy NIOD, Amsterdam

A multitude of signposts for Canadian regiments on the road to Nijmegen, immortalized in the poem of the same name by Canadian writer Earle Birney, mentioned in Professor Hans Bak's introduction in Part III. The front line of the Allied Forces was stalled between Nijmegen and Arnhem during the winter of 1944-45.

Copyright: Cas Oorthuys, Nederlands Fotomuseum, Rotterdam

Courtesy NIOD, Amsterdam

Princess Margriet, third daughter of Princess Juliana and Prince Bernhard, was born in Ottawa, 19 January 1943, in a hospital room that was declared Dutch territory. During World War II, the Dutch Royal family found safe haven in Canada. The painting in the background of the photograph (taken January 1944) depicts the *De Geuzen*, who were victorious in the 80-year-long war against the Spanish occupation of the Netherlands, 1568 to 1648.

Many Canadians lost their lives during heavy fighting in Holten. This simple sign (photo above) was later replaced by a marble memorial, "Their name liveth for ever more," at the entrance to the Canadian War Cemetery in Holten (photo right). Every year since 1991, candles are lit near the graves at Christmas (photo below).

Courtesy Frans van Cappellen

Groesbeek, the largest Canadian War Cemetery in the Netherlands. Of the more than 6,000 Canadian soldiers buried in the Netherlands, over 2,000 rest here.

Courtesy NIOD, Amsterdam

^ Fighting in Arnhem. During Operation Market Garden in September 1944, the Allied Forces were unsuccessful in liberating Arnhem. On 14 April 1945, however, Operation Anger achieved that goal.

Courtesy NIOD, Amsterdam

Harderwijk, the Veluwe, NL, where heavy fighting took place in April 1945. As Pieter Beelaerts van Blokland and Jan Piëst recall in their interviews, the liberation was an exciting time for boys, who enjoyed meeting the Canadian soldiers. Today, young people remain interested in veterans' stories, such as those told by Danny McLeod to Dutch students via Skype and webcam interview arranged by Bob Hofman.

Copyright: Cas Oorthuys, Nederlands Fotomuseum, Rotterdam

^ The Maple Leaf Bridge, built by the 1st Canadian Army at den Oever, a town on the western edge of the *Afsluitdijk*, a dike built across the sea separating the provinces of Friesland and Noord-Holland.

Courtesy Verzets Museum Friesland, Leeuwarden

^ April 1945. Two young Canadian soldiers guard a stash of rifles confiscated from the German army.

ˆ Delft, May 1945. Happy Dutch citizens welcome their Canadian liberators. Not only chocolate, cigarettes, and flowers were exchanged between Canadian soldiers and Dutch women, but also – as Eke Foreman-van der Woude recounts in her interview – eggs, soap, and offers of marriage.

ˆ Leiden, May 1945. Dutch children and a woman in traditional dress from the province of Zeeland pose with a Canadian soldier.

ˆ The Hague, May 1945. The first Canadian soldier arrives by motorcycle.

‹ May 1945. Liberation of Culemborg, in the heart of the Netherlands. Appreciative town residents carry a Canadian soldier on a "lap of honour".

Copyright: Kryn Taconis, National Archives, Ottawa

Amsterdam, 7 May 1945. Over 20 Dutch citizens were killed when Germans fired on the celebrating crowds in what has become known as the Dam Square Massacre. The official liberation took place on 8 May 1945.

Courtesy NIOD, Amsterdam

Amsterdam, May 1945. Signs such as this were hammered to trees and posted in windows throughout the city.

Copyright: Cas Oorthuys, Nederlands Fotomuseum, Rotterdam

Amsterdam, May 1945. Dutch citizens and a soldier pose before the archway of the *Admiraliteitsgebouw* [Admiralty Building], Amsterdam's former city hall, today the Grand Hotel.

Courtesy Flip Bool, The Hague, Private Collection

In *Holland and the Canadians* (Amsterdam: Contact Publishing, 1946. Eds. Major N. Philips, Canadian Army P.R. Services and J. Nikerk, Secretary of the Canadian-Netherlands Committee), Nikerk stated: "Canada will be among the first of the new ties we shall make overseas... perhaps many of our children, who are feeling the lack of space here in Europe, may in the future contribute to the development and prosperity of your people and country."

Courtesy NIOD, Amsterdam

Delft, Spring 1945. One of the many celebration dances organized throughout the country.

Courtesy Oorlogs- en Verzetsmuseum, Groningen

Groningen bride Betty van der Heide with her Canadian husband.

Courtesy *Koninklijke Bibliotheek*, The Hague

A series of humorous postcards about Dutch-Canadian relations during and after liberation at *Oranje bitter, Nederland bevrijd* ["Bitter orange, the Netherlands freed"] 28 April – 4 July 2010, a joint, bilingual (Dutch and English) exhibition of the *Koninklijke Bibliotheek* [National Library] and the National Archives of the Netherlands. In these selections, a dog takes credit for entwining another "wartime couple", and Canadian soldiers are pleased to "give a lift" to a young Dutch woman.

Rotterdam, 15 May 1951. Emigrants to Canada wait on the quay before boarding the S.S. *Volendam*. The grandparents of interviewees Kristen den Hartog and Malcolm Campbell-Verduyn left the Netherlands from this very quay in the 1950s.

Amsterdam, Schiphol Airport, 1957. Jelle de Boer and his family from the village of Langweer, the Netherlands, emigrate to Canada by Canadian Pacific air.

Amsterdam, Schiphol Airport, 1949. The majority of immigrants to Canada travelled by boat to Pier 19 in Montreal or to Pier 21 in Halifax. As this photograph shows, T. Loohuizen had his luggage sent by air to Macoll Farm, Inglewood, Ontario.

Montreal, Canada, 1950. Dutch emigrants aboard S.S. *Waterman* arrive at Pier 19 and are greeted by the Dutch Ambassador Dr. J.H. van Roijen and his wife Mrs. A. van Roijen-Snouck Hurgronje.

Montreal, Canada, 1947. The Dutch children, Piet Baan, Sari de Kooy, and Arie de Kooy, wait atop family luggage on the quay near the S.S. *Waterman*, one of the ships that brought Dutch emigrants to their new country.

Low land – High Hills by Andrea Stultiens. (Nijmegen: *In*/Druk, 2007) In British Columbia's Fraser Valley, the "Pitt Polder" [reclaimed farm land], created in 1951 by newly-arrived Dutch farmers, was photographed by Frits Gerritsen. Fifty-five years later, Andrea Stultiens's photographs of the Pitt Polder community record how Dutch immigrants became Canadian citizens, among them Henk (or, in Canada, Hank), who arrived in 1946.

Courtesy Frits Gerritsen

Copyright: Andrea Stultiens

Zwolle, NL, 31 January 2001. “Emigraria”.
An emigration fair for Dutch farmers and others in the agricultural field. This booth tries to attract Dutch farmers to Alberta, Canada.

Nieuwegein, NL, 3 March 2008. The 11th International Emigration Fair presents options to a generation interested in business, career, study, or volunteer opportunities abroad today.

Harry Witteveen, who left the Netherlands on the S.S. *Waterman* in July 1947, is one of seven portraits in the series, “Migrants”, at the Open Air Museum in Arnhem today (April 2010 until October 2010), produced by *Jippiejajeetv*, with research by photographer Anke Teunissen. Today, Witteveen is a successful breeder of Friesian horses on his farm in St George, Ontario.

The Hague, 24 October 1990. Dignitaries meet at the opening of the first European Canadian Studies conference, "Canada on the Threshold of the 21st century: European Reflections upon the Future of Canada". From left to right: H.E. Jacques Gignac, Ambassador of Canada; H.R.H. Princess Margriet; Dr. Cornelius Remie, president of the Association for Canadian Studies in the Netherlands; and H.E. Jeanne Sauvé, former Governor General of Canada, who delivered the keynote address. In the left background, Mr. A.J.E. Havermans, Mayor of The Hague.

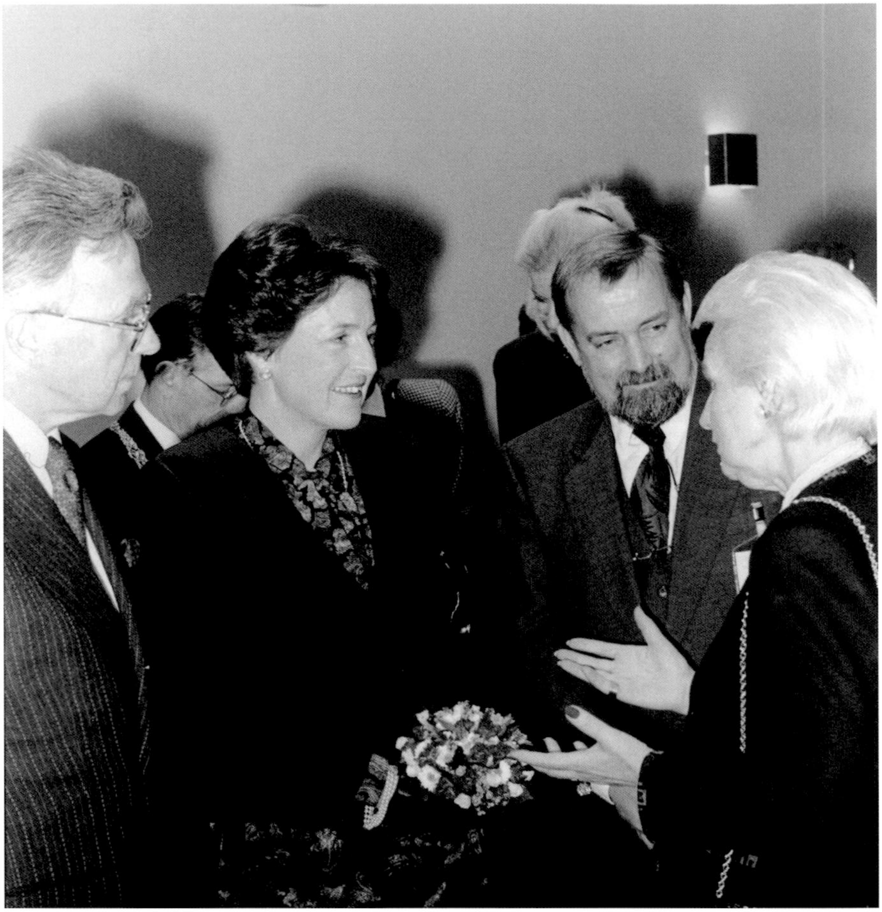

Copyright: J.J. Zeidner

Courtesy Rijksuniversiteit Groningen

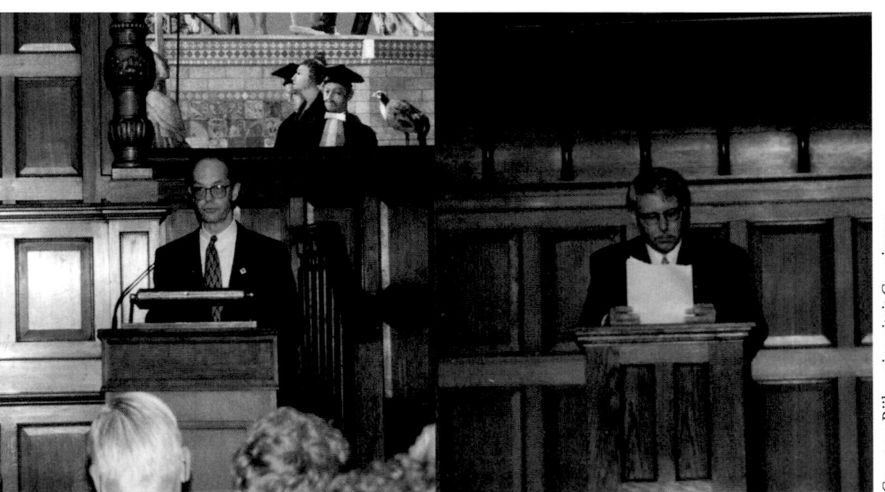

Groningen, 3 May 1995. H.E. Michael Bell, Ambassador of Canada, inaugurates the Chair in Canadian Studies at the University of Groningen. Professor Jaap Lintvelt of the University's Department of Romance Languages and Cultures held the Chair until his retirement in 2005.

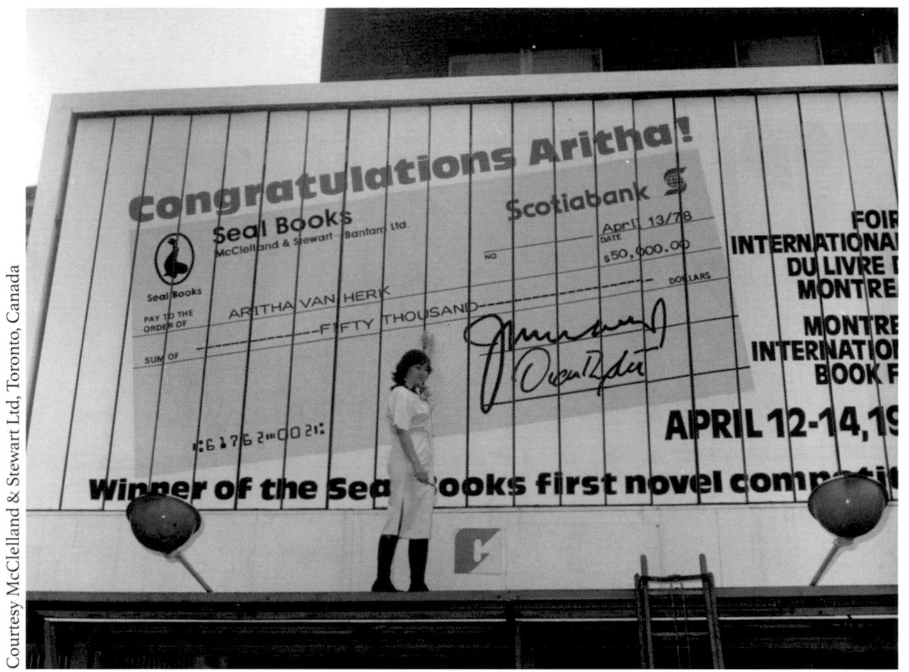

Courtesy McClelland & Stewart Ltd, Toronto, Canada

Writer Aritha van Herk, daughter of Dutch immigrants, won the prestigious Seal Canadian First Novel Award for her book *Judith* in 1978. Van Herk has explored the Dutch-Canadian immigration experience in fiction and non-fiction alike. Among others who have written on the subject – too many to name here – are Herman Ganzevoort (*A Bittersweet Land: the Dutch Experience in Canada, 1890-1980,* 1988*)*, Michiel Horn (*Becoming Canadian: Memoirs of an Invisible Immigrant*, 1997), Marianne Brandis (*Frontiers and Sanctuaries*, 2006), and Kirsten den Hartog (*The Occupied Garden*, 2008), interviewed in Part II.

Courtesy Melanie ter Meulen

Middelburg, 4 June 2005. Launch of *Building Liberty: Canada and World Peace, 1945-2005*, edited by Conny Steenman Marcusse and Aritha van Herk, at an ACSN conference that took place at the Roosevelt Academy, Middelburg, NL, on the occasion of the 60th anniversary of Liberation Day.

Copyright Anke Teunissen

Beginning in 1994, the Canadian Cultural Merit Award, which consists of a certificate and a work of art by one of Canada's Native artists, was presented biennially by the Canadian Embassy to individuals or organizations in the Netherlands that promoted Canadian culture in the areas of music, dance, theatre, film, literature, visual arts, and new media. The International Documentary Festival Amsterdam (IDFA) management team, Ally Derks and Adriek van Nieuwenhuyzen (photograph above) and Willemien van Aalst and Jolanda Klarenbeek, won the 2000 award. In 2006, the final award was presented to Cor Schlösser, director of Amsterdam's popular music venue, *de Melkweg*, which has hosted many Canadian bands, such as Arcade Fire, The Dears, Hot Hot Heat, and The New Pornographers.

Courtesy *de Melkweg*, Amsterdam

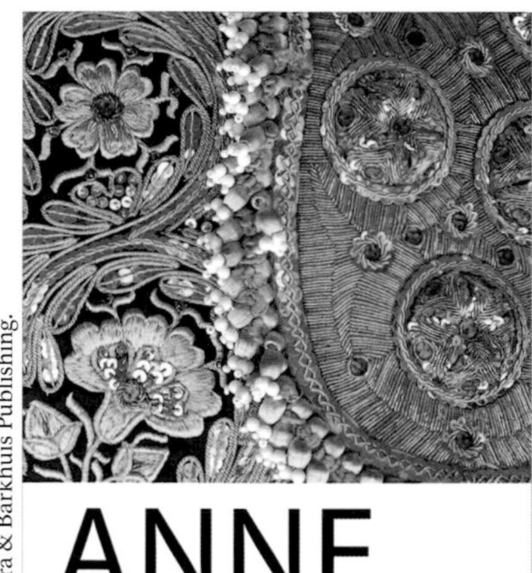

Courtesy Nynke Tiekstra & Barkhuis Publishing.

Dutch translator Pauline Sarkar has helped bring the work of *Québécois* writers such as Anne Hébert, Jacques Poulin, Marie-Claire Blais, Marc-Marie Bouchard, and Hélène Pednault, to the Dutch reading public. Her most recent translation is *Klatergoud* (Groningen: Barkhuis Publishing, 2008) – Anne Hébert's *Un habit de lumière* (Paris: Editions du Seuil, 1999).

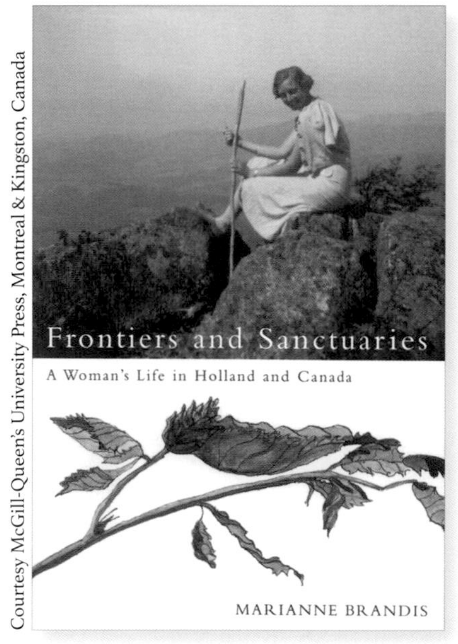

Courtesy McGill-Queen's University Press, Montreal & Kingston, Canada

Frontiers and Sanctuaries: A Woman's Life in Holland and Canada, Marianne Brandis's 2006 memoir of her Dutch immigrant mother's life.

SHIFT folder design: Adam MacLean

SHIFT, a multi-disciplinary arts festival in Amsterdam, 18-22 November 2008, organized by Jennifer Waring, Artistic Director of the Toronto-based Continuum Ensemble. The festival featured Canadian and Dutch music, film, literature, and visual art.

Crown Prince Willem Alexander and Princess Máxima, together with their three daughters, Amalia (left), Alexia (right), and Ariane (middle), cheer on Dutch speed skater Sven Kramer in the 5000- metre race, which he won at the Winter Olympics in Vancouver, 13 February 2010.

Princess Máxima (centre), Erica Terpstra, Chair, Netherlands Olympic Committee (left), and Jet Bussemaker, State Secretary of the Ministry of Public Health, Welfare and Sport (right), engage in lively conversation at a reception in the Holland Heineken House during the Winter Olympics, 17 February 2010. In her speech to veterans and wartime survivors on 18 February 2010 in Vancouver, Bussemaker, referring to the Second World War, stated: "Everyone, including the generations yet to come, is aware of this dark period in our world history. As State Secretary, I therefore see it as my duty to 'future-proof' the past. I must ensure that the memories live on, so that each successive generation can learn from your experiences. The young people of today and tomorrow must have the opportunity to ask questions, to find the answers to those questions and to draw their own conclusions."

ENTERTAINMENT COMMITTEE OF THE NETHERLANDS

CANADA
HOLLAND

SPORTSWEEK

17-25 NOVEMBER 1945

Friendly Meetings of Various Games	Vriendschappelijke Ontmoetingen op alle Sportgebied

IN HET GEHEELE LAND
PLAATSELIJK GEORGANISEERD
LOCAL ARRANGEMENTS ALL OVER THE COUNTRY

Canada Holland Sports week, 17-25 November 1945. After liberation, when Canadian soldiers stayed on to help the war-torn Netherlands, events such as these Friendly Meetings of Various Games, were organized all over the country for their entertainment.

Copyright: Robin Utrecht, ANP, The Hague

Courtesy Malcolm Campbell-Verduyn

While Dutch professional speed skaters, Sven Kramer, Jan Blokhuijsen, and Mark Tuitert, were blazing the track during the Team Pursuit at the 2010 Olympics in Vancouver, young and old amateur skaters in the Netherlands enjoyed the canals in the Alblasserwaard, near the Kinderdijk windmills.

Copyright: Robin Utrecht, ANP, The Hague

Canadian and Dutch speed skaters share the medal podium at the Vancouver Olympics, 19 February 2010. Canadian Christine Nesbitt won gold in the women's 1000 metres, while her Dutch competitors Annette Gerritsen (left) and Laurine van Riessen (right) took silver and bronze respectively.

Copyright: Robin Utrecht, ANP, The Hague

The Canadian men's ice hockey team in action during the final competition of the 2010 Olympic Winter Games in Vancouver. They won gold on 1 March 2010.

Nieuwdorp, NL, 30 October 2009. H.R.H. Princess Margriet officially opens the Zeeland Liberation Museum. From left to right: Jerzy and Naomi Traas, Octopus Primary School; Carla Peijs, Queen's Commissioner for Zeeland; H.R.H. Princess Margriet; Kees Traas, museum curator; E.J. Gelok, Mayor of Borsele.

Courtesy Bevrijdingsmuseum Zeeland/ Ad Kunst

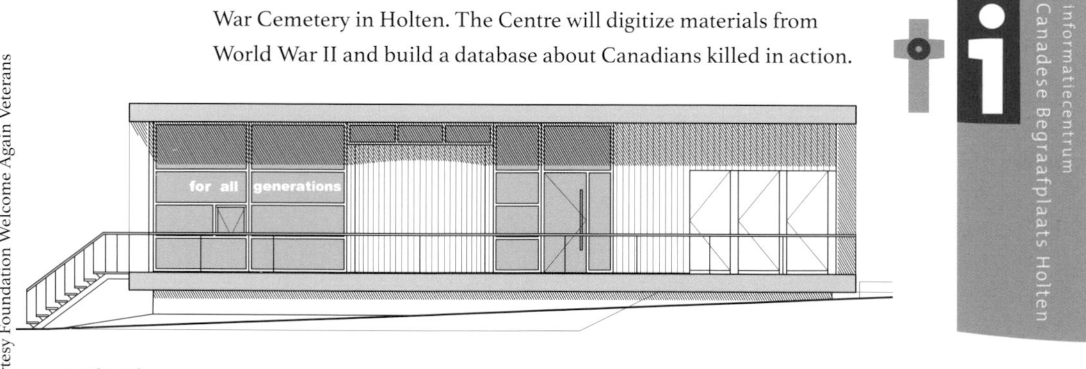

Blueprint and logo for the new Information Centre at the Canadian War Cemetery in Holten. The Centre will digitize materials from World War II and build a database about Canadians killed in action.

Courtesy Foundation Welcome Again Veterans

Copyright Anke Teunissen

Copyright Anke Teunissen

Members of Veterans Affairs Canada visit Bergen op Zoom, 22 March 2010, in preparation for the commemorative events of the 65th anniversary of the liberation in 1944 and 1945. In May 2010, 2000 Canadian students and their tour leaders, together with Canadian war veterans and their travel companions, partcipated in a memorable week of events organized by the national committee, "Thank you Canada & Allied Forces", and numerous organizations supporting Canadian war veterans. The events were attended by dignitaries of the two countries.

Canadian Forces officers Major Guy Turpin and Chief Petty Officer 1st Class (CPO1) Robert Horan at the Canadian War Cemetery in Bergen op Zoom, 22 March 2010.

Courtesy Anke Teunissen

Courtesy Anke Teunissen

Inscription on the gravestone of Private A.H. Balson, one of the thousands of Canadians who gave their lives for the liberation of the Netherlands: "Some day we'll understand."

Courtesy Anke Teunissen

Interviews

Olga van Ditzhuijzen, interviewer; Mark Baker, translator

Courtesy Anke Teunissen

“That people have lain down their lives, in a foreign country, for your freedom.”

Dr. Pieter A.C. Beelaerts van Blokland
President, “Thank you Canada & Allied Forces”

The Utrecht home of the president of the national committee, “Thank you Canada & Allied Forces,” is easy to find, thanks to a huge Canadian flag flying proudly from the balcony. “I must admit,” Pieter Beelaerts van Blokland explains as he opens the door, “it doesn’t hang there every day.”

There are, however, many Canadian paintings and photographs displayed in the home of this former Christian Democrat Minister of Housing, Spatial Planning, and the Environment (as well as former Mayor of Apeldoorn and former Queen’s Commissioner for Utrecht) that point to his affiliation with the Canadian liberators. Even the watch he wears is engraved with the emblem of the 48th Highlanders of Canada – a gift from the active veterans of this unit.

Since its foundation in 1978, “Thank you Canada & Allied Forces” has taken on the task of organizing invitations and commemorative events for the Canadian liberators every five years. The committee’s original aim was to avoid a conflict of loyalties for the veterans in the event that two municipalities decided to organize a parade on the same date. In addition, the committee advised municipal authorities on practical matters related to memorial ceremonies and wreath-laying.

Pieter Beelaerts van Blokland was born in 1932, so World War II and the liberation were very much a part of his formative years. When his father, who was Mayor of Barendrecht at the outbreak of the war, was ousted from office by the Germans, the family moved to “Keppel castle”, the family estate in the east of the Netherlands. Beelaerts remembers the war as an exciting time for a young boy who had to hide in the woods from the Germans when out after curfew. Beelaerts’s father made use of the difficult circumstances to teach his children about the arts of war by listening to the different kinds of explosions and fighting in the distance. “My father explained how the Allied troops were liberating us. We stood outside and he explained what was happening. 'If you can't hear any counterfire, that means the infantry is advancing,' this kind of thing." It was a crazy period, Beelaerts recalls. "One time, a Canadian suddenly ran into our dining room, and set up an anti-aircraft gun in the open window."

One day, the German tank that had been stationed behind the family home was suddenly gone – a sign that the war was over. "This was the start of a very exhilarating time for me as a young boy. I rode around in jeeps, was given uniforms, and hung around with the Canadian liberators morning, noon, and night. I collected the insignia of all the regiments that came through. Many years later, in Apeldoorn, I met one of the men who had taken me out in a jeep to collect eggs from the local farmers." The Canadians had set up camp on the grounds of the heavily damaged estate, in the Beelaerts's front garden. Officers were billeted in the house which, even with a leaky roof, offered more comfort than an army tent. "Things did go missing from the house every now and again. And the Canadians would lie around on the beds, with their boots on, that kind of thing. They were certainly no saints. Which is not really surprising, considering everything they had been through."

Following a political career during which he served as Minister in the Dutch government, Beelaerts was appointed Mayor of Apeldoorn in 1981. To mark the 40th anniversary of the liberation in 1985, the Mayor decided to organize a parade. "This had often been done before, in Amsterdam. But I always found this a little strange; most of the Canadians were interested in the places where their comrades were buried, such as Groesbeek and Holten."

Beelaerts had often had dealings with the veterans of the 48th regiment in particular, who had organized buses to Apeldoorn on their own. "This town is very important to many Canadians. A lot of heavy fighting took place here, in which they suffered heavy casualties." Beelaerts befriended the men of this regiment, and then decided to organize a big parade.

To provide accommodation for the roughly 3,000 Canadians making the journey in 1985, Beelaerts placed a newspaper advertisement appealing to local families to make their homes available. The response was overwhelming and many Canadians were able to stay with families in Apeldoorn. "It was really moving. For example, I met a woman who didn't speak a word of English, but who bravely managed to get by using dictionaries." Beelaerts points out that this led to new friendships between veterans and the residents of Apeldoorn. "The same lady was later invited to spend two months in Canada, to learn English."

In the town, a "Canadian Centre" was set up, where veterans who took part in the liberation could meet one another and make contact with the local population. "We had such a great time," Beelaerts remembers, "with music, singing, and dancing deep into the night." The parade itself was extremely impressive, Beelaerts relates. "The Canadians said they had never seen so

Courtesy N. Vendelbosch

Apeldoorn, NL, 2005. Canadian veterans participate in the 60th anniversary of Liberation Day parade in vehicles arranged by the association, "Keep them Rolling" (KTR), and accompanied by music bands from home and abroad. Apeldoorn's first major Liberation Day parade took place in 1985, through the initiative of Dr.P.A.C. Beelaerts van Blokland, president "Thank you Canada & Allied Forces".

Dr. P.A.C. Beelaerts van Blokland, President "Thank You Canada & Allied Forces", lays a wreath at the Canadian War Cemetery in Holten.

Courtesy A. Hartkamp.

many Maple Leaf flags in one place before!" Beelaerts also points out that many residents of Apeldoorn lined the route with exceptional enthusiasm. This was a major difference from other commemorations, organized principally for and by the veterans themselves. "For the Dutch people present, it was as if they were experiencing the liberation of Apeldoorn all over again." A wave of euphoria washed through the town; as one Canadian veteran described it to the Mayor at the time: "Mister Mayor! I feel like I am 20 years old again!"

Beelaerts views the parade as a breakthrough. "You see how happy this kind of recognition makes people. Not that they have been underappreciated, but this mainly took the form of military medals and the like. What we did was a direct expression of gratitude by the people themselves. That is what made it so special."

Following the success of the parade in Apeldoorn, Beelaerts became involved with the national committee "Thank you Canada & Allied Forces". This organization is now concluding its work; in five years' time, most of the veterans will be too old to make the trip to the Netherlands. And those devoted veterans who do come over now know the way well enough, Beelaerts adds. "The commemorations will continue, but will have to take another form. And thinking about freedom will continue to flourish in the contact and exchange projects between young people. The realization that people have lain down their lives in a foreign country for your freedom – this should not pass unmarked."

...

Courtesy Anke Teunissen

“The Men of Maple Leaf”

Jan Piëst
Commemoration Chronicler

Ten scrapbooks full of letters, photographs, newspaper clippings, and reminiscences are displayed on a special table in the library in Haren, a small community just south of the city of Groningen. Together, they form a collection of expressions of thanks from Canadian war veterans who were stationed in this northernmost province of the Netherlands during the last months of World War II.

Often in a shaky hand – one envelope is addressed simply to “The Mayor of Haren, Holland” – the veterans describe how happy they were to receive “The Groningen Scroll”. This poem of thanks, penned by Haren resident Jan Piëst, is titled “The Men of Maple Leaf” and is printed on a stately scroll, with a picture of Groningen’s Martini Church and the seal of the Municipality. The poem has now found its way into the homes of some 1,200 Canadians who took part in the liberation of Groningen.

In the photographs enclosed with the letters, the elderly veterans proudly pose with their wives – and the scroll – in their Canadian living rooms. The captions often state their appreciation of this expression of thanks, while insisting that their deeds were not so exceptional. “You people were just like us,” one former liberator writes. Piëst and his wife have forged many new friendships on the basis of these contacts.

Jan Piëst (82) experienced the liberation of the city of Groningen as a teenager. For two long days, he lay on the floor of his family’s upstairs apartment, while Canadian tanks rumbled through the streets and the Germans fought their final battle. Seven months previously, the teenaged Jan had been forced by the Germans to dig pits as traps for the advancing Allied tanks. One rainy November day, Piëst worked thigh-deep in a water-filled pit and caught pneumonia. The doctor managed to stretch out the recovery period long enough for Jan not to have to return to digging pits, and so, from the window of his parents’ home, he was able to watch the first Allied tanks enter the city.

An exciting time then dawned for the young Piëst; days were filled with looking at tank wrecks and searching for spent cartridges in the streets. "The atmosphere was euphoric," Piëst recalls at his home in Haren. "That feeling of eternal gratitude is engraved in my memory." Most of the Canadians were billeted in schools, and many spent their time swimming, and in the pub, while others had to advance on to the German front. "There were some really tough characters among them, even though these Canadians were only 20 years old. They had been through so much, had seen some really awful things."

Piëst was impressed by the Canadians' somewhat lackadaisical attitude. "They weren't tightly disciplined like the Germans; they were really nice guys." His sister was given a bar of chocolate by a Canadian soldier. She has kept it all these years, untouched; that chocolate is now 65 years old.

In the years that followed, Piëst did not actively think much about the war, until the big celebrations in 1985 for the 40th anniversary of the liberation. Canadian veterans came to stay with Dutch families, including in Groningen. "Captain Clayton Miller stayed with our neighbour. She asked me to help him look for a family that lived in a small village and had given him food and shelter during the last months of the war." Piëst became fascinated by the stories the veteran told. "I sat talking to him for hours, then finally got in my car to go and look for that family in the village."

The farmhouse was no longer there; new houses had sprung up on the site. Two hours of questioning local residents revealed who the family must have been, and in the end Miller managed to visit them. And it didn't end there. "He then wanted to see the place in Germany where his army friend had been shot dead by a sniper, after the liberation. I drove there with my wife to take photos of the place, which was close to a castle." Miller was extremely thankful. A year later, the Canadian captain passed away.

From that moment on, Piëst's interest in Groningen's Canadian past grew by the day. "I thought that not enough attention was being paid to what Canadians had done for Groningen. I wanted to fill this void." In retirement, Piëst wrote his poem, "The Men of Maple Leaf", as a means of expressing his appreciation by presenting it to the old soldiers. "Not to the high-ranking officers, no; but rather to the ordinary, rank-and-file soldiers." In 1995, the poem was presented at the opening of *Bevrijdingsbos* [Liberation Woods"], a new park planted with maple trees on the outskirts of Groningen. It went down extremely well, recalls Piëst: "The poem really struck a chord." In three cases, the scroll bearing the poem was even placed alongside the coffins of deceased veterans. It is also on display in Groningen's Martini Church and at the Canadian Embassy in The Hague.

Piëst is also regularly approached by Canadians with questions and requests. One former soldier, for example, wanted to know what had become of a young girl whom he had accidently hit with his jeep. Mrs. Piëst

Groningen 1945.
Young Jan Piëst
gets a close look
at an army tank.

A Canadian war veteran with the "Groningen Scroll".

Courtesy Jan Piëst

laughs: "My husband is like *Spoorloos.* ["Without a Trace", a Dutch television program that reunites people who have lost touch with one another]; once he gets his teeth into one of these cases, he just won't let go."

The Piësts are an inexhaustible source of anecdotes told to them over the years by Canadian veterans. To keep these alive, in 2005 Piëst wrote *The True Watcher* in English about his memories of the war, the liberation, the scroll, and the many meetings he has had with veterans. "You could say Canada has pretty much dominated my life over the past fifteen years."

The Men of Maple Leaf

Bold they were, the combatants we knew
How deep our sympathy for them grew
South they came and fought their way
Memory engraved is that glorious day
Lives squandered, precious blood shed
Our want for freedom was finally met
There was scarcely time to fraternize
The battle went on, at high a price
In the actions brave ones would fall
Facing their losses the men stood tall
It took three days to clear the town
Dislodging the enemy beyond our bounds
Stricken by panic some fled to the shore
Deserted or were scattered to the four
Many fighting wearied, surrendered fast
Our war torn hometown was freed at last
Smouldering ruins were marking the place
Where battering damaged her ancient face
Peace returned, the yoke of war was gone
Thanks to the Canadians, a tough task done
To commemorate them we dedicate a forest yet
Maple leaves fell for us, lest we forget

J. Piëst

...

Courtesy Anke Teunissen

“The moment he removed his helmet, I knew: he’s the one for me.”

Eke Foreman-van der Woude
War Bride

In May 1945, the airstrip at Eelde exerted an irresistible attraction to the inhabitants of this small village in the Dutch province of Groningen. The Canadian Second Infantry Division used the ravaged space as a base for its tanks, and a number of regiments of the liberating army made camp there. The people of Eelde were well aware that a little bit of well-placed flattery would usually produce a packet of tea, or a bar of soap, or chocolate from the hardy soldiers.

Nineteen-year-old Eke van der Woude and her friend Klaasje were among those who liked to come and gawk at the soldiers. Klaasje’s parents raised chickens and the girls would try to swap eggs for soap from the soldiers. One day, two friendly young servicemen had some soap for them, but it was inside their tank. Would Eke and Klaasje like to join them for a cup of tea? The teenagers needed no second bidding, and they quickly divvied up the young men between them. “That one is mine,” Eke told Klaasje. But at that moment the other soldier – good-looking 22-year-old Eldon – took off his helmet. “No, hold on, I’ll take this one!” Eke whispered to Klaasje. “Luckily, she was an easy-going girl, and didn’t mind. And that’s how I met my husband,” Eke Foreman-van der Woude – now 84 years old – reveals on the telephone from her home in Oshawa, Ontario, a town in the vicinity of Toronto. “Those were the days,” Eke reflects aloud. She vividly recalls the dances, organized every Sunday afternoon for the Canadian soldiers. “There was always a band, and we drank tea; there was never any alcohol.”

Eldon was Eke’s very first boyfriend, and their relationship quickly deepened. “I eventually fell very much in love, and we were married on 24 December 1945.” This was no easy endeavour, involving miles of red tape, permits, and paperwork. “I remember him calling me on a Saturday to tell me we could get married on the Monday. My neighbour had saved a piece of good material all through the war for a special occasion. She let me use it for a bridal gown, on the condition that I send her some fabric from Canada. My older sister spent all that Sunday sewing the dress for me." Eke danced with Eldon in the same dark red, shiny dress on their 50th anniversary. Of course, Eke's family did not really want to let her go, the youngest of seven children. "I had to go," she explains, "I thought I would never be able to marry anyone otherwise, I was so madly in love." Following the wedding, Eldon was transferred to Apeldoorn, and from there he was to leave for Canada, "so we spent our honeymoon in Apeldoorn!"

The plan was for Eke to follow her husband to Canada after the summer. With the demobilization of Canadian troops, many army ships returning to the homeland doubled up as "bride ships", carrying some 44,000 European women and 21,000 children to a new future in Canada or the USA. The ship Eke boarded in Rotterdam was called the Lady Rodney, a passenger ship that had brought Canadian soldiers to Europe during the war. It was a "dinky little ship," compared to the majestic Queen Mary, to which the women transferred in Southampton for the long crossing to Halifax, Canada.

With some 2,000 young women on board, the crossing was one big party. "It was a great journey. Every day, there were theatre performances and dancing. We Dutch girls performed a clog dance; we'd never done that before. God only knows where we got them from!"

Having arrived in Halifax, the women were taken on to their final destinations by a special train that stopped in every town where a bride was due to meet her Canadian husband. Sometimes, sadly, the platform was empty – not all the women were as lucky as Eke, whose Canadian lover immediately gathered her up in his arms.

Eke never met the women from the boat again. She is also not a member of the "war bride clubs" that shot up relatively quickly to provide practical support to the women. "I lived in such a small village; there just weren't any other Dutch people or other war brides to set up a club with."

Eke did, however, recently have a remarkable encounter. "I went to the shopping mall, which was closed – this was strange, because the shops are often open 24 hours a day here. There was another woman standing there, and we got talking. I asked her: 'Are you Dutch?' 'Yes,' she replied. 'I'm a war bride,' I said. Turns out, she was too! In fact, we had been on the same boat, on the same day. Truly bizarre." Since then, she sees her new friend, Corrie Clark, regularly. They usually speak English, as it feels more comfortable. But when she talks about the old days, Eke intersperses her sentences with Dutch expressions, in a slight Groningen accent. She did not teach her sons to speak Dutch, though. "When he was little, the eldest would shout out proudly: 'I am not a Dutchman, I am a Canadian!'" Eke laughs. "Now, they think it's a shame I didn't press them, but I couldn't *make* them speak Dutch, right?"

Courtesy Eke Foreman-van der Woude

Eke van der Wouden and her Canadian solider, Eldon Foreman.

Eke and Eldon Foreman celebrate their 50th wedding anniversary in 1995, Eke wearing the same dress that she wore on her wedding day in 1945.

Courtesy Eke Foreman-van der Woude

Eke was fortunate to be able to pick up English very quickly: "After three months, I pretty much had the basics. My husband always made fun of my pronunciation of the 'w', but I still don't know what I'm doing wrong." Eldon never talked about the war. "I know he fought in Italy, and that they lost three tanks there. He also never wanted to go back to the Netherlands. He went over with me once, but that was it. Too many memories, I think." Eke does know one story from Eldon's war years, however. "He was the driver of the tank, and the gunner sat behind him. So the bullets literally whistled past his ears. One time, the gunner was cleaning the gun, when it unexpectedly went off. The bullet passed straight through Eldon's helmet. He slumped forward, but luckily was completely unharmed. A few centimetres lower, and he would have been dead. The gunner was traumatized by the incident for years after." During a reunion with Eldon's regiment in 1995, Eke and Eldon met the wife of the gunner concerned. "She told us that he had never got over it. In his mind, he had killed Eldon."

Eldon passed away eight years ago, and Eke still misses him every day. "He was such a sweet, good man. Remember, not every war bride was as lucky. Some girls were met only by an empty platform, some didn't recognize their husband without his helmet on, or were disappointed by their new love without the uniform."

In spite of her 84 years, Eke's impish giggle is still that of the bright, adventurous young woman that she must have been back in the 1940s. She went skiing in Quebec every year up to the age of 78, and she still immensely enjoys Canada's vast natural beauty, saying with great enthusiasm: "I just *love* Canada." Eke has just one sister still living in Eelde, and of course has nephews and nieces in the Netherlands. But would she consider returning? "Never. It's so different, I couldn't live there any more. Good lord, the shops are not even open 24 hours a day!"

...

Courtesy Anke Teunissen

"Your father was a Canadian."

Mary Derr-de Jong
Liberation Baby

Her name is Mary. But precisely why Dutch Mrs. Derr-de Jong was given such an Anglo-Saxon name, she is not entirely sure. Is it because her father was one of the Canadians who liberated the Netherlands at the end of World War II? Perhaps it was simply a popular name in the heady months following the liberation. Or, could it have something to do with her Canadian grandmother, who is also called Mary? Could Mary's mother have known this, and named her baby after the mother of her liberator lover? No one has wanted to answer these questions in the past, and now there is no one left who can answer them; both Mary's Canadian father and her Dutch mother are deceased.

Mary Derr-De Jong (64) is one of the 8,000 "liberation babies" who were the result of brief encounters between Allied servicemen and Dutch women at the end of the war. Ever since she can remember, Mary was told that her father was a Canadian soldier. It was no secret, "but apart from that, my mother's lips stayed tightly sealed. 'Your father was a Canadian, and that's all I have to say on the matter,' she said."

During the first post-war years, baby Mary and her 25-year-old mother lived in Aerdenhout, with Mary's grandparents. Four years after Mary's birth, her mother married and had another two daughters and two sons. Curiosity about her biological father, however, always lurked at the back of Mary's mind. "I was very curious, particularly as a teenager. But I didn't even know where to start looking," Mary says, seated at the dining table in her home in Heerhugowaard, in the province of Noord-Holland. Her husband sits by the window reading a newspaper, now and again adding a detail to the story. Mary never had a photograph of her long lost father, so she used her imagination. "Could he be looking for me? Maybe one day he will turn up at the front door?" She always pictured him as a young man. "Every war film or television series reminded me of my mysterious father. Was he one of these brave fighting men?"

After chancing upon a radio interview with Canadian "liberation children" researcher John Boers, Mary, then aged 40, began seriously to look for her biological father. She contacted the Canadian Association of Liberation Children (disbanded in 2006), which gave her advice on how to start the search and shared stories of people in similar situations. When the first big Canadian liberation parade was held in Apeldoorn in 1985, Mary handed out flyers bearing her appeal to hundreds of veterans.

To mark their 25th wedding anniversary, Mary and her husband took the whole family on their first ever trip to Canada. Once there, Mary realized that she was looking for a needle in a haystack. Canada is pretty big. "It's 240 times the size of the Netherlands," Mr. Derr says triumphantly, as he pours the coffee. The task was made even more difficult by another unhelpful factor, Mary explains. "My father's surname was 'Miller,' an extremely common name in Canada."

It is likely that Mary's mother met her Canadian lover at one of the many dances held in the wake of Liberation Day. Mary made enquiries throughout Aerdenhout and the surrounding area in search of clues. With a great deal of effort, and some help from her aunt, Mary learned that her mother only discovered that she was pregnant after her Canadian lover had left. Mary's father probably never knew that he had a daughter in the Netherlands.

In an era when computers were still a novelty and the internet only a pipe dream, amateur detectives like Mary were reliant on information from the Red Cross and local telephone books. Letters took ten days to arrive, never mind the time it took for a reply to come back. Another obstacle was Canada's strict privacy legislation, which made it very difficult to access information on former servicemen. "One time, in a museum, I dared to say that I was looking for my father, who was one of the Canadian troops that liberated the Netherlands," Mary says. This statement did not go down well. "One poor man had the fright of his life. He assured me at least ten times that he was not my father! So I never did that again. Another time, I approached some veterans in Apeldoorn with my question, and they said: 'Well, I must be your father then!' I took a more cautious approach after that."

Mary collected telephone books from various places in Canada. "I wrote letters, which I then copied and sent to thousands of people. My aunt said that my father came from Ontario, but even Ontario is incredibly large." Many of the letters came back stamped "return to sender." Some people responded with long epistles telling their own stories, which was good of them, Mary observed, but did not help her much in her search.

While on holiday in Canada, Mary and her husband visited numerous museums and archives. "We found lots and lots of books and names. But how do you know when you have found the right name?" They also visited local "legions" – associations where veterans from particular military units regularly meet. "I put up flyers there," Mary says, stressing that she was always discreet. "I didn't want to cause any family ructions. We always said we were looking for old friends. The aim was never to find my father at any cost at all."

Mary's search lasted for 14 years. During that time, every letter that dropped onto the doormat represented a brief spark of hope, followed by inevitable disappointment. "This kind of search drains your energy; it is very emotional. On the one hand, there is fear. What if we find him and he doesn't want to know me? What if he is dead?" On the other hand, the dream of one day being reunited with her father kept Mary's hope alive.

In 1999, Mary and her husband decided to scale down the search. After all, the chances of finding her father were dwindling all the time. "Until one day, while we were on holiday in Austria, we got an email from John Boers. He had found my father!" But how he had found him was unfortunate: a newspaper obituary. Too late.

Courtesy Mary Derr-de Jong

Mary Derr-de Jong's Canadian father.

"Of course, I was disappointed by this; I would never be able to speak to him in person. On the other hand, this made it easier to contact the family. His wife, to whom he was already married during the war, had also passed away." There was a photograph, and "it was immediately clear as day," says Mary. It was as if she was looking into a mirror. She was her father's daughter.

John Boers approached the family carefully to tell them about the "lost daughter" far away in the Netherlands. Fortunately, the family was happy to be contacted. The ball was then in Mary's court.

"The first conversation was really scary," Mary recalls, but after some preliminary small talk, Mary's brand new half-sister asked her if she would like to visit Canada. "We were planning to do so anyway," explains Mary, who, quite apart from the search for her father, had fallen completely in love with the wild beauty of the big country. "We went over that summer and met 40 family members. It turned out that I have four sisters, who received us with the words 'Welcome to the family.' My eldest sister is three years older

Mary Derr-de Jong with her four Canadian half-sisters.

than me, and there is another who is just eight months younger. We have all discussed it with one another. Of course, there's no excusing what he did; but then again, it was wartime."

Mary immediately got on well with her four sisters. "Funnily enough, of the five of us, I resemble our father the most." Her new Canadian family has also told Mary that her facial expressions and character are very reminiscent of their late father. Ever since, Mary and her husband have visited their overseas family every year for a holiday or for Christmas. The house in Heerhugowaard is full of photographs of Mary's Canadian sisters, alongside enlargements of holiday photographs set against the stunning Canadian landscape. Mary and her husband have now seen almost the entire country, from Niagara Falls to the Rocky Mountains, but Mary's favourite destination is her eldest sister's ranch, where she likes to horse ride. She suspects that she has inherited her love of nature from her father. "It's hard to explain. But whenever I am in Canada, it somehow feels like home."

...

Courtesy Mary Derr-de Jong

Mary Derr-de Jong and her husband, vacationing on Vancouver Island, June 2009.

Courtesy Kristen den Hartog

“I am incredibly proud that *Oma* and *Opa* dared to take that step.”

Kristen den Hartog
Granddaughter of Dutch Immigrants

The small bungalow belonging to Canadian writer Kristen den Hartog’s *Oma* and *Opa* was in the village of Aylmer, Ontario. To her, their house always seemed to have materialized from another world. “It even smelled different. They dressed differently, and spoke English with a thick accent,” the author of *The Occupied Garden* (2008) recalls over the telephone.

In 1951, Dutch market gardener Gerrit den Hartog and his wife Cor boarded the steamer *Volendam*, along with their five children, on the way to an unknown future in Canada. In her book, which she wrote with her younger sister Tracy Kasaboski, den Hartog traces the life story of her grandparents, chronicling the crisis years in their home town of Leidschendam, their experiences during World War II, and finally the crossing to the far-off “promised land” and their struggle to build a new life.

Her Dutch roots have always fascinated den Hartog. On the website for her book, she describes her grandparents’ house as follows: “Lace curtains hung in the front window, and meals were taken at a heavy oak table with claw feet. Noses wrinkled, we tasted sour buttermilk, dark crumbly bread, and horsemeat shaved paper-thin. After supper, *Opa* read the Bible in Dutch – a beautiful sound made more so by the softly guttural language we didn’t understand.” Now, den Hartog reads aloud to her six-year-old daughter Nelly (named after *Oma* Cornelia) from Dutch picture books – not that either of them actually speaks the language, but trying to pronounce the funny looking words from Rien Poortvliet’s *Welterusten Kleintje* [“Sleep tight, little one”], for example, and to guess their meaning, is a great source of shared fun.

Like her grandfather before her, den Hartog is keen on gardening. She was therefore pleased when, several years ago, a magazine asked her to write an article on the subject. The only problem was that her tiny flat in Toronto looked out on nothing more than a postage-stamp-sized yard full of stones. So she decided to write a story based on her grandfather’s reminiscences. “It got a lot of reaction,” den Hartog says. “People found it a moving story, and my literary agent asked whether I would be interested in writing a book about my family history." But den Hartog, author of the novels *Water Wings* (2001), *The Perpetual Ending* (2003), and *Origin of Haloes* (2005), was reluctant to make the leap from fiction to non-fiction. She discussed the proposal with her sister Tracy, which led to the idea of them co-writing the book. "This made it a lot more manageable, and it was a good opportunity to work together. Tracy had always written stories, but had never pursued writing as a career, so this was a perfect chance." The book has since been translated and published in the Netherlands as *De kinderen van de tuinder.*

While *Opa* Gerrit worked in a nursery tending plants and flowers, *Oma* ran a travel agency and a dry goods shop, selling products from Holland. "Rolled-up posters from all over the world sat in the basement of their house," den Hartog writes, "but *Oma* and *Opa* had rarely travelled themselves – only, really, to go back to where they'd come from, though they'd never imagined that would be possible when they'd left the Netherlands."

The family had experienced some horrible incidents during the German occupation of the Netherlands. Kristen's father and uncle were seriously injured just months before the war ended, when a bomb landed behind their house. Her father, Koos, lost a leg, and Uncle Gert, an arm. These and other tragic events were hardly ever discussed by the family, however. In her grandparents' house, only one box containing a few objects served as a reminder of the war years: it contained Gerrit's and Cor's identity cards, photos from the years in Leidschendam, and a postcard from a Jewish friend who had fled to Switzerland during the war.

Den Hartog's grandparents both passed away long before the book was written, so the two sisters relied principally on the memories of their father, uncles, and aunt. Nevertheless, the experience of the book gave the sisters the impression that they had come to know their grandparents better. The relationship between their father and his siblings was also strengthened through the intensive contact, much of which was by email. This led to a huge stack of correspondence which, according to den Hartog, is a real "family treasure trove."

Of the five children, the eldest daughter, Rige, finally returned to the Netherlands ten years ago. The youngest son, Nick, also lives in the Netherlands; he simply stayed on after having been educated there. Emigration has had a range of effects on the children: Niek became Nick; Gert became Gerry; Rige, who was fifteen years old when the family emigrated, wrote reams of letters back to her friends in the Netherlands, while the boys were keen to master their new language in Canada. Kristen's father Koos decided to switch his name to James, and later to Jim, and started writing his surname DenHartog. "He immediately wanted to identify himself as a Canadian." His marriage to Kristen's mother, a Canadian of English descent, ran aground, and he eventually swapped his house for an itinerant existence on a sailing boat with his new wife, who happens to be from the Netherlands. They even speak Dutch to one another.

Courtesy Kristen den Hartog

Opa den Hartog's nursery and garden in Leidschendam, the Netherlands, before the war.

Dutch culture has left a strong imprint on the family. Kristen's uncles are passionate about sailing, and Uncle Nick in the Netherlands has a century-old *skûtsje* [a converted flat-bottomed barge] from Friesland. Flowers are also a common link; before she began writing full-time, Kristen worked as a floral designer and realized how Dutch that industry is, even in Canada.

After the book came out, den Hartog discovered how common it was for other families to avoid discussion of the war years. Its publication led to a stream of responses from immigrants, and children and grandchildren of immigrants, who tell their own personal stories on *The Occupied Garden*'s website. Den Hartog is also regularly invited to give lectures or readings to Dutch book clubs and organizations. "A little while ago after one such evening, a man approached me in tears because the book had confronted him so strongly with his own experiences." She points out that immigrants experience their past in a completely different way than those who remain in their home country. "They have been cut off from their country of origin and history. If you stay in the same place, you see your history all around you and gradually process this; but many immigrants, especially children, feel abruptly uprooted from their familiar surroundings."

The sisters den Hartog wonder what their grandparents would have thought of the intimate family portrait they have drawn. "*Opa* and *Oma* were very private people, very traditional. They might have wanted us to change the names, out of modesty." She stresses that she wanted to write a respectful account. "I am incredibly proud of *Oma* and *Opa*, that they dared to take the step to emigrate. It was a really courageous decision for such conservative people, to make the crossing," Den Hartog explains. Looking back, she wishes that she had asked her grandparents more questions while they were still alive. She hopes that her book will lead to more people being curious about their own family history, and working to preserve memories for future generations.

...

Courtesy Anke Teunissen

"We were *Ajax* supporters without ever having seen a game."

Malcolm Campbell-Verduyn
Grandson of Dutch Immigrants

With his head of blond hair and love of cycling, Malcolm Campbell-Verduyn (25) could easily be taken for a full-fledged, finger-in-the-dike, cheese-eating Dutchman. Yet, as his double family name indicates, this graduate in political science is both Dutch and Canadian in background. His grandparents, *Opa* and *Oma* Verduyn, emigrated from Amsterdam to Canada in 1953, settling in the city of Peterborough, Ontario, where *Oma* Verduyn still lives today. *Opa* Verduyn passed away several years ago but Malcolm has vivid memories of his grandfather. "He had tiny little stars in his eyes: scars from stone splinters, caused by working as a stone mason." The Verduyns' grandson now wants to reverse the long boat journey undertaken by his grandparents and move to the Netherlands – no longer by boat, of course!

For Malcolm, emigration is not such a big step. "Growing up, my family moved quite a bit," he says, relaxing in an east Amsterdam café. "We lived in a number of different cities in Canada, but also in France for a while." When Malcolm was 18, he came to Europe on a family holiday, which took in London, Paris and, of course, the Netherlands. "Straight away, I thought Holland was really cool. I just loved it. The windmills, and all the bicycles."

A few years later, he had the opportunity to take part in an exchange program through his Canadian university. "I spent a year studying in Amsterdam, in 2005-2006. Because I speak French, my professors in Canada thought that I should go to Paris, but I wanted to study in Amsterdam. I'd already lived in France. I really wanted to come to the Netherlands."

At the University of Amsterdam, Malcolm took every class on Dutch society that he could. "The attitude here is really refreshing. Of course, there are social issues – such as drugs and prostitution – which the country is trying to solve in its own way. This was also an important reason for coming to Amsterdam; I wanted to study this political vision, and coming from Canada it was more interesting for me to study what appeared to be a much different legal system."

In Amsterdam, he met his girlfriend, Lorette, a young and sporty Dutch woman pursuing her degree in film studies. "I knew that I had to go back to Toronto to finish my Bachelor's degree, but when Lorette came along, I decided to take my Master's degree in political science – in Leiden. I wanted to see more of Holland, outside of Amsterdam. I wanted to live in a smaller Dutch centre. Amsterdam doesn't represent all of the country; here, everyone immediately speaks English to me. In Leiden, that doesn't happen nearly as often."

So Malcolm moved to Leiden, while Lorette was based in Amsterdam. "Yes, it came as a surprise to her, too! But I'd cycle up to Amsterdam every weekend to be with her." Eh, by bicycle? "It's a three-hour ride, that's not so bad. I thought it was a good way to get some exercise and explore the Dutch countryside. I started doing it in the summer and really got into it." When it got to October, though, Malcolm soon discovered the true hardship of his bike tour. Like a real Dutchman, with a long-distance skating endurance gene, he struggled on. "The wind can be very biting in the flat *polder* landscape ... especially when it's in your face and you are carrying a heavy backpack full of books. I often arrived tired and sweaty and sometimes I was late for class."

The former student was struck at how close together everything is in the Netherlands. "You are always cycling past villages and buildings. There are no really large, uninhabited spaces, like the forests of Canada: over here, there is always a signpost to somewhere."

As an adolescent Malcolm grew more and more curious about his background. "Questions like 'Why is my brother so tall? Why do we drink so much milk at home? Why do we eat cheese and *vla* [a kind of cold custard with different flavours]?' occupied me more and more." In high school, he signed up for courses in German since there were no courses in Dutch. "I thought, German's not so different from Dutch. But it ended up only confusing me more when I got here. I noticed that it is often better to speak English here, rather than German! I would say *ich habe* instead of *ik heb*; not everyone appreciated that."

In spite of his Dutch grandparents and the fact that his mother was born in Amsterdam, Malcolm has not yet mastered the Dutch language, but he is taking lessons and improving rapidly. "My mother understands and speaks Dutch well enough, but it's no longer her first language." He was always fascinated by "those crazy sounds" his grandparents would sometimes produce. "For example, I was intrigued by words like *gezellig* [cozy, fun] and the strange intonation of the Dutch language."

Malcolm is aware of many Dutch traditions from his family life. "We had *stroopwafels* [waffle-shaped treacle cookies] in the house – often long past their sell-by date because they had to be imported – and I was given sandwiches with *hagelslag* [chocolate sprinkles] to take to school. They were very popular with my classmates." The family always celebrated *Sinterklaas*

Courtesy *Oma* Verduyn

Opa and *Oma* Verduyn and family pose for a pre-emigration photograph.

[5 December, the feast of St Nicholas], complete with *pepernoten* [button-size gingerbread treats]. And it supported *Ajax*, Amsterdam's *voetbal club* [soccer team]. "My father sometimes visited Amsterdam for work, and he would bring back *Ajax* hats and scarves. We were *Ajax* supporters without ever having seen a game. Everyone in Canada watched ice hockey, but we were Dutch soccer fans."

Now, Malcolm wants to get his Dutch citizenship. Unfortunately, he was born six months too early to acquire Dutch citizenship through his mother, and is currently one of the "latent Dutch" (children born to a Dutch mother abroad before 1985 cannot claim Dutch citizenship. This does not apply to children born of a Dutch father). Malcolm's younger brother and two sisters all have Dutch passports. Malcolm remains optimistic, however; changes to the law were recently approved by the parliament of the Netherlands.

Does he feel Dutch now? "In Canada, no one has just one identity," he reflects. "My father, for example, comes from Scottish and French background." Malcolm does see some clear parallels between his two home countries. "Both the Netherlands and Canada are pretty small countries, in terms of population. And the people of both countries share a largely relaxed and generally tolerant attitude. They may not rule the world, but they don't start a lot of wars either. And that is not a bad thing, if you ask me."

...

Courtesy Anke Teunissen

"I am 'new', and in Rotterdam everything is also new."

André Gingras
Director, Dance Works Rotterdam

If André Gingras gets his way, Rotterdam's shopping streets will soon be overflowing with modern dancers: productions on the square in front of the theatre, instead of in the theatre itself. It is the rawness of this port city – this immigrant city on the River Maas – that appeals to Gingras, that he wishes to use as a backdrop for his choreography, and that reminds him, somehow, of the Canadian industrial port city of his birth.

Choreographer André Gingras has lived and worked in the Netherlands for 12 years now, and was recently appointed director of Dance Works Rotterdam. Born in 1966 in the city of Hamilton, Ontario, Gingras's French-speaking family moved from Quebec to this Mecca of the steelmaking industry in search of a better life. Virtually everyone who lived there at that time worked in steel, and Gingras's school friends all saw themselves making a living in this industry.

But Gingras's mother, who, with his grandparents, raised young André, saw things differently. "She always encouraged me to do what I really liked." Because he was academically strong, and loved reading and acting, André left Hamilton to pursue Theatre Studies and English Literature at the *Université de Montréal*. He originally wanted to train as an actor, but slowly discovered that his heart really belonged to dance.

Having obtained his Bachelor's degree, the 21-year-old Gingras signed up at Toronto's dance academy. "I was really way too old already. I had lessons with women who had been learning ballet since they were tiny. It was really hard work." After Toronto, Gingras headed straight for New York City. "Back then, in the 1990s, that was *the* place to study dance, and there was still enough work, although it was already getting tougher." The city, and life in neighbourhoods such as the West Village and the Lower East Side of Manhattan, gave Gingras a terrific boost. "New Yorkers are smart, clever, and very hard workers; they have very high expectations. This really formed me."

From 1991 to 1996, Gingras worked with a range of different dance companies. Nevertheless, he did not really see a career for himself as a dancer in New York. He observed how difficult it was for older, more established dancers to make ends meet. When one of his dance contracts expired, Gingras decided to spend some time travelling. He auditioned for dance productions in Germany and Switzerland, eventually dancing his way through Europe, before finally settling in Amsterdam. "There are all these workshops and production houses just for dance in the Netherlands; that's really unique," Gingras explains. "It's a luxury situation. Even in New York, there is less money for dance. I have lived in a lot of countries and seen a lot of different situations, but the efforts made for art – and for dance in particular – in the Netherlands are far greater, even, than in other European countries." This prompted Gingras (who spoke remarkably good Dutch throughout our long conversation) to learn this new foreign language. He now thinks in English, swears in French, and dreams in Dutch.

Gingras was able to sleep on a friend's couch in Amsterdam for a while. "Then I did some auditions and got a long-term contract with Dutch-American choreographer Arthur Rosenfeld. This immediately got me off to a booming start, and I was then able to get a foothold in the Netherlands." According to Gingras, the fact that this small country does so well on the international stage deserves greater attention. "You people should drop this modest behaviour!" This is one of the many parallels between the Netherlands and Canada that Gingras has discovered over the years. "Both countries are very modest about their cultures; both the Netherlands and Canada are dominated by their neighbours: the USA and, in Europe, Germany and France."

So has he noticed any special connection between the Netherlands and Canada? "I have always felt welcome in the Netherlands. Perhaps this has something to do with the liberation? In any event, the Dutch make a clear distinction between Americans and Canadians. 'Ooh, you're Canadian? Good', people say. Almost with relief."

Gingras has been creating choreography, characterized by comical moments and contemporary themes, since 1999. His dance piece *CYP17* had its première at the CaDance Festival in The Hague, and won a host of glowing reviews. "I was immediately established as a choreographer, with my first piece, which was a bit strange," Gingras laughs. "I just wanted to create a work for myself, and suddenly I was called choreographer." Three years ago, Gingras decided to stop dancing and concentrate all his energies on choreography, which has now led to his appointment as director of the prestigious Dance Works Rotterdam company. "It was really an honour to be given this position, and I'm really looking forward to it."

His diary is full: Saturday, a production in Paris; Sunday, a performance in Rotterdam; and Monday, management training in Stuttgart. But Gingras feels a special affinity with Rotterdam: "I started out there as a student with Dansateliers and now I'm the director. Also, the style I was trained in corresponds to the atmosphere of that city." Gingras's works are raw, urban, layered, and highly physical. "I am 'new,' and in Rotterdam everything is also new. Whereas Amsterdam has all these marvellous historical buildings, in Rotterdam it's different. You are forced to start something new, because the city was bombed so badly. This has created a new feel, exciting, and very inspirational." Gingras is "an immigrant in a city of immigrants," he says. His greatest desire is for Rotterdammers to adopt the Dance Works company as "one of their own," even if the boss is a Canadian. "The guy with the funny name," Gingras adds.

Courtesy Lukas Wassmann

Amsterdam, *Julidans* Festival, 2009. Gingras's choreographies are characterized by energetically explosive dance and humour. In *Idoru Solo's*, the commercialization of the body is performed.

He sees a clear line running through Canadian art. "Take filmmaker Atom Egoyan, the director of *Chloe*, for example. That's a typically Canadian film, in my opinion. The makers are very friendly and warm, but there is a kind of darkness and multi-layered nature to their work. I sometimes hear the same thing: why do I make such dark, nasty works, when I'm a nice guy otherwise?" Whether it is some shared Canadian spleen, or a collective depression caused by the long, dark winters, Gingras would not like to say. "It has struck me that the arts disciplines are more distinct in the Netherlands; each has its own colour, they are very diverse. I can't really find any shared characteristic. In Canada, most art tends towards the innocent-looking, with a dark undertone."

So, Gingras fits into the Canadian art tradition – but does he still feel Canadian? A deep sigh escapes the choreographer's pursed lips. "It's a funny thing, but sometimes I really feel like an outsider. I understand what Canada is all about, and I feel a great attachment, but nevertheless, I have somehow left it behind. That's painful. On the other hand, I miss the incredible beauty of nature there. When I had just moved to the Netherlands, I once suggested to a friend 'Let's go out to a nice place in the wilderness.' But that just doesn't exist here. A few years ago, I went with some of my family to a national park close to Montreal and when I looked at the map, I suddenly realized that the Netherlands could fit into that park three times over."

Gingras finds it difficult to say whether he will ever return to Canada. Showing a rather Dutch side to his character, he drily replies: "I have a lot of pension savings here." However, he adds, "I still work in Canada a lot; I just

"Multiple
Queen Liz"
Anatomica # 3.
Rambert Dance
Company,
U.K. 2010.
Choreography
by André
Gingras.

Courtesy Chris Nash

created a piece in Montreal and I have a lot of contact with Canadian artists." For example, he recently persuaded choreographer Dave St. Pierre from Quebec to create a piece for Amsterdam's *Julidans* international summer festival. Gingras was closely involved as artist in residence at Amsterdam's music venue, *De Melkweg*, where, in 2006, director Cor Schlösser was awarded the Canadian Cultural Merit Award for his pioneering role in discovering alternative Canadian pop music.

Gingras has also picked up the Dutch commercial and entrepreneurial *nous*. "Compared with other countries, the Dutch are much more accessible; directors of big institutions are much more approachable here. Try making an appointment with the director of the *Centre National de la Danse* in Paris: good luck!" He aims to be a typically Dutch, accessible director. "We need to give art back to the community. I want to put Dance Works Rotterdam at the heart of society, instead of in an ivory tower. I think the Netherlands is ready for this kind of model. I can't wait to get started. This is exactly what I want."

...

Courtesy Anke Teunissen

Maple syrup

"We use it literally almost every day."

Sandra van Rijn
Maple Entrepreneur Abroad

It happens all the time to Sandra van Rijn, when she presents her company, Maple Abroad, at trade fairs and the like: an older Dutch man or woman will see the Canadian maple products on her stand and start talking about World War II. "They can be really moving stories, very personal. It always really strikes me that Canada still touches people like that."

Sandra runs a business selling Canadian maple products from her home on the outskirts of Leiden – mainly the famous maple syrup, but her online store also offers herbal teas, wine, cookies, maple butter, jelly, and chocolate "moose droppings". In addition, Sandra has entered into a deal with the Dutch supermarket chain C1000, as well as several restaurants, and the Food Village supermarket at Amsterdam Schiphol Airport, to sell her Maple Abroad products.

Sandra (53) is married to a Dutchman, Cor van Rijn. They met in Glasgow, where he was working and she was completing her studies in architectural and construction engineering. At that time, the end of the 1980s, jobs for architects were hard to come by, and Sandra and Cor stayed in touch to keep one another informed of work opportunities: "We were pen pals," Sandra recalls.

The friends subsequently roamed all over Europe, their story becoming every bit as complicated as those of many immigrants to Canada. In fact, just to make it even more complicated, Sandra was not actually born in Canada. "My mother is rather a romantic soul, and wanted her child to be born in New York. She thought: 'It looks good in a passport.' She therefore swapped Montreal for Manhattan for just one day, and that's where I was born. Yes, it is a bit strange. I didn't see much of the city," says Sandra, with one of her hearty laughs.

Cor went to work in London with a friend, and Sandra left for Paris, where her brother was employed along with many other Canadians on the construction of Euro Disney. Several months later, Cor followed Sandra, and in 1993 they married in Paris. Job opportunities in Europe were still not abundant, and Cor was offered work in Saudi Arabia. Due to visa complications, Sandra was unable to join him. “So that was it: ‘bye Cor.’”

She retrained as an architect for Eastern Europe, and was sent to St Petersburg to restore old buildings and palaces. Cor again followed, and after three years – following some “small problems with the Russian mafia,” and an unfortunate accident befalling Sandra (“I fell through a rotten floor; it could have easily been a lot worse”) – the couple decided to settle in the Netherlands. “Which was handy, because Cor’s family lives here, of course. I wasn’t really too bothered where I was. We’ve now been living here for 13 years.”

All the travelling had to come to an end sometime, and they both wanted an environment in which they could raise a child safely. When their daughter, Liesbeth, was born in 1996, and Sandra wanted to spend time at home with the baby, she started her maple syrup business “out of boredom” and to keep in touch with Canada. She was surprised that the famous syrup was so difficult to find in the Netherlands, when for Sandra it is an essential kitchen ingredient. “We use it literally almost every day; as a marinade for spare ribs, as a sweetener in coffee or tea, and in cakes. You could compare it to honey in that sense.”

Sandra has set out a number of samples of her products on her kitchen table. A huge can containing four litres of maple syrup steals the show. “These sell really well, I swear! It keeps for a very long time, of course, but there are ‘expat’ women here who place a regular order for these giants.” It doesn’t seem cheap, at some 20 Euros a litre, but this is not because of the import duty. Sandra explains: “It is a very painstaking process. You need 40 litres of maple tree sap to make one litre of syrup.”

Cor’s and Sandra’s big dream is to own their own maple tree woodlot back in Canada. “Then I’ll get a lot of workers in to tap the sap for me,” Sandra laughs. She can already picture it in her mind’s eye, the only problem being that there are many rules and regulations attached to buying property in Quebec, the Mecca of maple syrup. But it should be possible, one day – perhaps when Cor has finished his housing project in Leiden. Sandra has also picked up her career as an architect again, establishing the firm Simply Architects with a friend in 2006. She likes the Netherlands: “It’s fantastic here!” But her love of nature is difficult to indulge in the scant Dutch countryside. Fortunately, Sandra’s and Cor’s house has a view over open fields, which, appropriately enough, are home to Canada geese.

“We lived in the *Statenkwartier* area of Leiden for seven years, a real working class neighbourhood. The women across the street would sit outside for hours with thermos flasks of coffee, gossiping about ‘that strange woman over there;’ that was me.” Sandra wanted to swap the former working class house in town for something a bit more out of town. “We chose this

Courtesy Anke Teunissen

spot especially because of the protected nature reserve opposite. Not for the house – we are still renovating. But, you see that ditch? Last winter, I skated on it with my daughter!"

Sandra has been organizing trips and meetings for the Canadian Club of the Netherlands for years now. A Canadian pavilion was also created for the celebration in Oosterbeek of the 50th anniversary of the liberation. "That was a big success," Sandra remembers. She points to the importance of "little Canada", so close to the ambassadorial city of The Hague, where numerous Canadian "expats" live. "Many young mothers spend quite a few years at home alone. We help each other out: looking for a French *crèche*, for example, or talking about cultural differences. Canadians are by nature extremely polite and can be shocked by Dutch directness. For example, if you walk into a shop and ask about a particular product, you might be told curtly: 'Look, it's right there!' I don't have a problem with it, I find it funny."

Sandra feels 100% Canadian, in spite of her international background. "It's wonderful that you are welcomed with open arms when you tell people where you are from." It seems that the experiences of World War II are still as fresh as ever. This was also the case when she met her parents-in-law for the first time. "They were really sweet, partly because they have such a good relationship with Canadians, because of the war. My mother-in-law is my best friend."

...

Courtesy Anke Teunissen

Courtesy Gerry Blom

While Sandra van Rijn supplies maple products to the Netherlands (photo opposite page), Gerry Blom's Holland Food Imports supplies traditional Dutch products to Canada's east coast Maritime provinces, Nova Scotia, Prince Edward Island, and New Brunswick.

Courtesy Gerry Blom

Courtesy Anke Teunissen

“He lived in a tank for one year.

That fact made a big impression.”

Bob Hofman
“Echoes” Project Coordinator

It is four p.m. in the village of Tubbergen, close to Almelo, in the east of the Netherlands, and a low-slung sun casts long shadows across the fields that run alongside the new buildings of Canisius College. In a darkened classroom in this modern secondary school, supervisor Bob Hofman is calling, “Good morning Danny!” into a computer monitor. “Can you hear me?”

For a moment, making contact with 87-year-old Danny McLeod in Kingston, Ontario, resembles attempted communication with a space shuttle on its way to Mars. However, turning the computer off and back on again and fiddling with some cables eventually pays dividends: a larger-than-life-size image of McLeod appears on a screen on the wall. He is dressed for the occasion in an army beret and the medal-laden uniform of the South Alberta Regiment.

Six grade nine students following the school's bilingual Dutch-English curriculum have given up their afternoon to webcam with a Canadian war veteran. The group has deliberately been kept small, to keep the session from becoming too unmanageable.

The students take turns at the computer, reading out questions they have developed in advance, serious expressions on their faces. The tension in the classroom is palpable, but McLeod looks relaxed and amused – in spite of having seen the communication program Skype for the first time last week, and having never used a webcam before. He answers the students' questions – quite possibly for the 100th time in his life – with patience. McLeod gives his carefully formulated views on modern warfare. “The situation in Afghanistan is completely different. This is more of a political war. People are still getting killed, but not nearly as many as in wars in the past. And the army makes an effort to educate the locals, to provide infrastructure, and to help the people run their own affairs. It's not a war like World War I and World War II. Our modern media mean we can be informed instantly of everything that is going on. This was not the case back then. In those days,

Courtesy Anke Teunissen

Bob Hofman sets up the Skype and webcam interview with Canadian war veteran Danny McLeod.

we didn't even have television. We can now zoom in on a single casualty, who is then immediately flown back to Canada, and buried with full military honours," McLeod notes. "Plus, these soldiers are away for short periods of time. Six months on the job, and then they come home. We were out there for five years."

Why did he decide to join up? "A very close pal of mine, who belonged to the same boxing club, said to me one day: 'I am taking the next troop train. Are you gonna come too?' And I said yes. So I left school, in grade 11, and we went off together." All those years away from home, all the misery of the war, does he not regret it? "Absolutely not. Just to liberate a city and see all the people so deliriously happy ... it's great."

When two Canadian exchange teachers enter the classroom, it turns out that the veteran also knows his ice hockey, and a real Canadian discussion about the formations and strategies of their favourite team crackles through the classroom. After 45 minutes, the session is brought to a close. "That was really brave, talking about the war like that," one of the students observes. "Great that he made the time to do this for us," comments another. The students are clearly impressed by this live link to a witness to world history.

The Skype session is part of the educational project "Echoes from the past, poems for the future," marking the 65th anniversary of the liberation of the Netherlands by Canadian and other Allied Forces. The project aims to

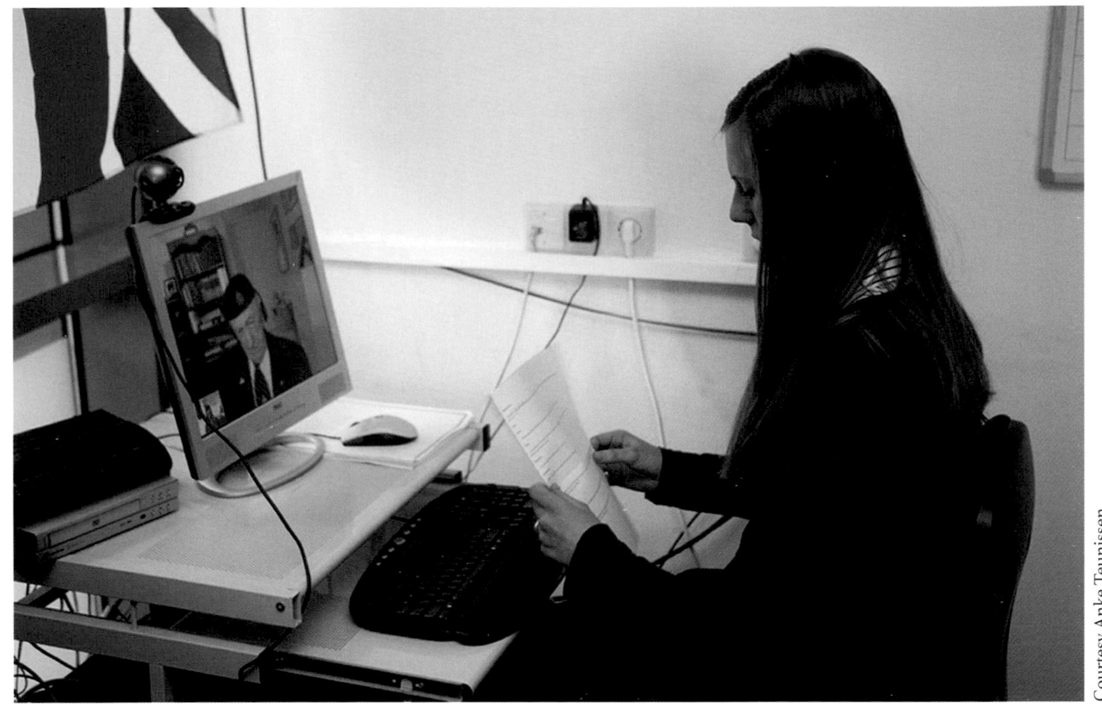

Courtesy Anke Teunissen

Canisius College student on Skype and webcam with Canadian war veteran Danny McLeod.

acquaint young students with the personal stories of war veterans, to keep the memories and the history alive. Bob Hofman is the driving force behind the "Echoes" project. He spent 25 years teaching audiovisual media at a secondary school in Uden, in the Dutch province of Brabant, and has always been a great advocate of the application of information and communications technology in education.

"We were the first school with a website, back in 1994," Hofman states proudly. He was surprised by the limited use made of digital technology in lessons. "For six years, I watched students learn to program using just one Macintosh computer and a turtle: the program Logos. What is that all about? Children want to communicate. You can clearly see this, now. Children sit together all day in the classroom, then when they get home they immediately go online to chat with one another." Hofman believes that schools should make use of this communicative urge. "Let them chat to their peers on the other side of the world. They can really learn something." This forms the basis of the Global Teenager Project, an initiative of, and co-production with, the International Institute for Communication and Development (IICD) in The Hague, with which Hofman has been associated since 2000.

Hofman facilitates "Learning Circles", a form of virtual cooperation in which teams of students from different countries exchange information and experiences on a given theme using text messaging, chat, and video. The results are collated on a web page to which everyone can contribute. This includes the "Echoes" project, which Dutch and Canadian students join in search of stories about the war. This year's project is a follow-up to successful efforts in 2005, when students held a video conference with veterans and expressed their own thoughts on World War II in poems.

Children's sense of wonder is Hofman's major motivating factor. "I still find this one of the most beautiful things in the world: this urge and will to learn." History teacher Maurits Kamman has been teaching in the bilingual program for four years and wanted to look at World War II through Hofman's project. "He is a typical example of an inspirational teacher, someone who tries to bring history up close," says Hofman. "You can fill a school with all the latest technology, but at the end of the day it's all about what you do with it." He points out that teachers are sometimes afraid they will be made redundant by the new forms of education, such as e-learning and online teaching materials. "While in fact, teachers have never been more important than now: it is they who have to guide students through a world overflowing with digital opportunities."

Making World War II tangible to younger generations is an ever greater challenge, now that most of those who actively took part have died. "We are really noticing it now. Five years ago, there were more than 80 veterans we could approach for a project; now, there are just three." Hofman hopes in future to be able to make use of as many video and audio "canned memories" as possible. "But we have to start collecting them now. Children want answers to questions such as: 'Did people go to school during the war? Were there football clubs?' 'I don't know,' I tell them. 'Go and ask your grandparents.'" This can lead to awkward situations: overenthusiastic children storming retirement homes in search of people with stories, or taking mischievous photographs at war memorials. "This can be a little overwhelming," Hofman laughs, but he sees it as a good sign: "At least they are getting involved." His aim is for children to learn firsthand what war really means. "Walking barefoot on the street, because you have no shoes anymore. Or being icy cold in the house because there is no fuel for the heating."

Hofman, too, always learns something new, he says. "During the chat, McLeod compared the sending of troops to Afghanistan with his own experiences. 'Our boys' are sent there for six months, in relative comfort, by plane, and then get six weeks leave before having to return. McLeod sat in a tank for a whole year. That is something I will never forget. Five men living together in a tank all year round: that is war."

...

The "Echoes" Project

Illustrations of two poems written by a Dutch and a Canadian student
http://echosfromthepastpoemsforthefuture.pbworks.com/All-the-poems

The friendship through the fence

Best friends forever
Blocked by the fence
Best friends forever
Stopped by the marching soldiers.
Best friends forever
Blocked by the Fürher
Best friends forever
Stopped by their differences.
Best friends forever
No longer blocked by the fence
Best friends forever
A friendship that no one could ever end.
Even older sisters
Even adults
Even soldiers
Even difference
Even death.

By Jacquelien
(Sg. St.-Canisius, Almelo and Tubbergen,
The Netherlands)

Remember

They Protected our Country,
They Protected Us,
They helped us get freed,
They helped us get rights,
They Left their family for us,
To fight for us,
To try and stop the bombs and guns,
So we remember,
Our special heroes,
That risks their lifes,
That gave us freedom,
And safed our lifes.

By Amanda
(Miramichi Valley High School,
New Brunswick, Canada)

* Poems are presented here as written by the students.

Courtesy Lia and Helena Dell'Orletta

"We feel it is important

to forward these memories to the next generation."

Lia and Helena Dell'Orletta

Daughter and Mother Explore a Family War Story

Helena Dell'Orletta (née Brouwer) asked her father, Tom, whether she could call her daughter Leah, after her aunt Lia, who was killed in the Netherlands by a bomb during World War II. However, she wanted to use the more common Anglo-Saxon spelling. Grandpa Brouwer agreed, but said: "For me, she will always be Lia, L-I-A."

So the baby girl was named Lia, spelled L-I-A. "Not always handy, a name you always have to spell out for people," 16-year-old Lia Dell'Orletta says, grinning through the webcam from her home in Barrie, Ontario. But it does make her a little bit special, and she is very much in awe of the story behind her first name.

It was the end of February 1945 when, during the intense aerial combat above The Hague, a bomb fell behind the Brouwer family's house. Eight-year-old Tom and his 11-year-old sister Lia were sitting in the living room peeling tulip bulbs, which – along with sugar beet – were a common emergency foodstuff during the Hunger Winter. The explosion threw them both to the floor. Everything went dark. Tom was able to save himself by quickly running from the house, together with his parents and his five other siblings. For Lia, it was too late. She had been hit in the stomach by shrapnel and died within minutes. Bombs fell even on the day of her funeral. As the congregation left the service, some members were hit by falling rubble. Lia's body was taken to the cemetery, some three kilometres away, by transport tricycle.

This is the story Lia Dell'Orletta's *Opa* told. According to Lia and her mother Helena, *Opa* frequently shared his memories of the war with his family. "He remembers going to the soup kitchen to get soup, and spilling some on the way home," Helena says. "The people waiting in line dived down and scraped the spilled soup up from the cobblestones with their spoons, they were so hungry. He can still hear that sound, to this day."

Helena's mother, Lenie, met Tom in 1956. She was one of a family of 13 children that had plans to emigrate to Canada. The plans became reality in 1959 and Tom had to choose between coming to Canada to marry Lenie

Courtesy Dell'Orletta family

The Hague, 1944. Lia's great-aunt Lia Brouwer and her brothers Tom and Ed in front of their home.

Courtesy Dell'Orletta family

Lia and Tony Dell'Orletta visit their great-aunt's grave in the Netherlands in 2004.

or losing her. He came to Canada. They were married a year later and in 2010, their 50th anniversary will be celebrated with children, grandchildren, and relatives – both Dutch and Canadian. Lia is proud of the Dutch branch of her roots. "I don't know anyone who has such an elaborate and interesting heritage. I have had the opportunity to tell my friends about my *Opa*'s past, but it wasn't until we took history classes about World War II that they understood the context of it all. Many kids were extremely surprised to learn about the Nazis and the holocaust, and kept on talking about it long after school. It is valuable to know someone who has a connection with the real experience. Nobody else knows what it was *really* like."

In May 2010, Helena and Lia spent 12 days taking part in the Victory in Europe Tour, a tour of World War II memorials specially organized by the educational travel organization, EF, to mark 65 years since the liberation. The trip included London, Amsterdam, and Bergen op Zoom, as well as the town of Vimy in the north of France, site of the World War I Canadian National Vimy Memorial, and finally Paris.

Helena and Lia became inspired in 2005, on a trip to visit family in Italy and the Netherlands. Lia still remembers her first impression: "The accent was pretty shocking to me, everybody talked like *Oma*!" And, naturally, huge quantities of *pannenkoeken* [Dutch pancakes], *hagelslag* [sweet sprinkles], and *poffertjes* [mini-pancakes] were consumed. "It was great; we recognized a lot of the buildings from *Oma*'s old photos."

Oma went along too, and rode a bicycle again for the first time in many, many years. "She really enjoyed speaking Dutch to the shopkeepers, and eating herring and ripe cheese." Helena noticed that the cousins who accompanied them often referred to World War II. "They would say 'before the war, there was a different building here,' things like that. Or you could still see bullet holes in a wall. In old cities in Europe, everything is reminiscent of the war.

I once asked an old farmer in Canada what he had experienced of the war. 'Well,' he said, 'the church bells rang when it was all over.' Then they knew no more men would be sent to the front. But there are no physical reminders."

The family also visited Aunt Lia's grave, and the Canadian War Cemetery in Bergen op Zoom. "That made a huge impression," Helena says. "When we got home, it turned out that this was the memory that stayed with us most."

Courtesy Dell'Orletta family

Bergen op Zoom, 2004. The Dell'Orletta family visit the Canadian War Cemetery. From left to right: Helena, Tony, Lia, Dino.

When Helena read in the newspaper that an Ontario high school teacher was taking his class on a tour of war memorials, she decided to do the same. "We're building memories. We suddenly realized the impact of history when we were there five years ago. Now we feel it is important to forward these memories to the next generation, so Lia will remember this link. So she keeps the connection." Lia nods, and says: "From a Canadian perspective, we have hardly any remnants of the Second World War, apart from propaganda posters calling for men to join the army."

At the same time, in Barrie, which has a large Dutch community, there is no escaping Dutch cultural heritage. Lia tells me about the retirement residence on her street, which is home to mostly elderly Dutch residents. "On 5 May, Dutch Liberation Day, they all fly the Canadian flag. And there is a kind of mini-festival, with a stall selling *kroketten* [croquettes with meat and potato filling] in buns. And a huge banner saying: 'Thank You Canada for Liberating Holland!'" Helena smiles: "This type of thing also helps raise awareness of the war years. Even if it's just neighbours passing by, asking themselves what on earth is being celebrated."

Helena has noticed an increasing need among the older generation to share stories. Together with her husband, Dino, she runs a company that supplies hearing aids, so they naturally have many older customers, including World War II veterans. "When I see their date of birth, I always ask them where they served. One customer told me that he had been a navigator in a fighter plane, and got 'so tired' of being shot at all the time, that he wished that he would be shot down. He told this story in such a nonchalant, dry way, I was quite struck by it." She believes that many of her customers like to talk about their war experiences. "There is so much still to say. People have only realized this since the 50th anniversary of the liberation, which was celebrated so extensively in the Netherlands. We also had parades here, and heard stories about how warmly the Canadians were received by the Dutch. Since then, there has been a lot more recognition and awareness."

...

Essays

Introduction

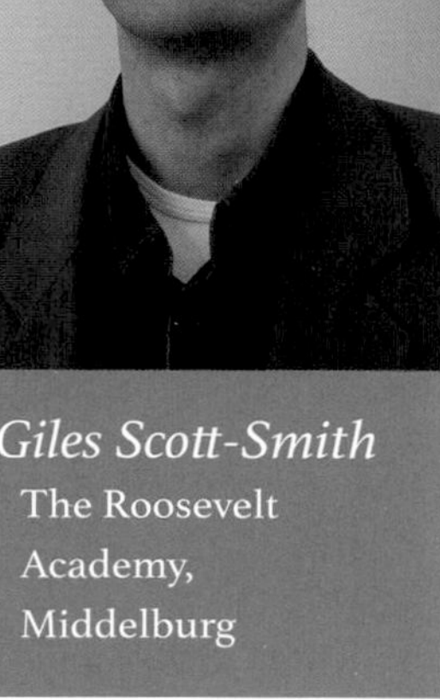

Giles Scott-Smith
The Roosevelt Academy, Middelburg

In the increasingly multipolar world of the 21st century, like-minded nations will need to work together effectively in order to achieve their foreign policy goals. While there are few political certainties in this situation, there are more opportunities for building coalitions and achieving results. As the following five essays show, not only are Canada and the Netherlands adept at operating in these circumstances, they also share many interests. Canada is said to be the most multilateral nation in the world, in terms of its involvement and engagement in international institutions and agreements – and the Netherlands comes in at number two. There is thus a great deal to be gained by working together in the fields of security, financial management, international law, transatlantic trade, and climate change.

While both Canada and the Netherlands are somewhat overshadowed by larger, more powerful nations, they have been able to successfully profile themselves as champions of a whole array of causes for the betterment of the rest of the world. They are both economically integrated into regional frameworks, Canada in the North American Free Trade Agreement (NAFTA) and the Netherlands in the European Union (EU). The Dutch and Canadians have invested heavily in maintaining their status as "knowledge economies", enhancing their value in negotiating agreements with rising powers and emerging markets. Through the causes they support and the professional expertise they can provide, they have secured access to the "top tables" of global diplomacy.

Key agreements have been made with Canadian "trademarks", such as the Montreal Protocol of 1987 that phased out ozone-damaging chemicals, and the Ottawa Treaty, banning the use of landmines. The Hague, the legal capital of the world, as Arlinda Rrustemi's essay on the International Criminal Court shows, is justifiably renowned as the world centre for institutions of international law (van Krieken, 2005). Canada initiated the G20 in 1998, and the Netherlands has contributed a great deal of financial expertise since the institution came of age, to coordinate responses to the global credit crisis from 2008 onwards. With the next G20 meeting in mid-2010 in the hands of Canada as host, it is to be hoped that Dutch participation will continue. As Moritz Baumgaertel states in his essay, the sheer scale of the Dutch banking, insurance, and pension fund sector should justify their inclusion. In terms of development aid, both nations belong to the Organization for Cooperation and Development's 22-member Development Assistance Committee, a forum for sharing information and discussing effectiveness. Both Ottawa and The Hague have recently initiated major reviews of their development aid policies in order to ensure greater effectiveness in recipient nations. The Netherlands provides around 8% of its Gross National Product to Official Development Aid (OECD Statistics), one of the few countries to top the UN's suggested goal of 7%. Meanwhile Canada has more than tripled its aid from $1.5 billion in 2001 to $4.7 billion in 2008. Lastly, the impact of climate change is not lost on either government, leading to further opportunities for collaboration, as Jacqueline Breidlid argues in her essay.

Yet it is not only policies that bind the two nations together. Emigration to the New World began in the 17th century, and Canada has been a specific destination for many Dutch settlers since the 19th century. The 2006 census in Canada revealed just over a million people who recorded themselves as being of Dutch origin, out of a total of 32 million (Statistics Canada). 150,000 Dutch immigrated to Canada in the two decades following the end of World War II, looking for a new life. The Dutch integrated well into Canadian society, quickly adopting the language and cultural traditions of their new country; according to Herman Ganzevoort, the main remnant of "Dutchness" in Canada is pockets of Calvinist Protestantism (Ganzevoort 1988). The two nations have more in common than simply policies.

Considering this background, it is not so surprising that both Canada and the Netherlands feature strongly in the various subject fields covered at the Roosevelt Academy. In the International Relations courses that I teach, for instance, my classes have examined the role of NATO and the security policies of its member nations in Afghanistan. The 3D approach – Defence, Development, and Diplomacy – was pioneered by Canada in the province of Kandahar and developed further by the Netherlands in Uruzgan, as described by Djeyhoun Ostowar in his essay. This has given the two nations a vanguard role in formulating a kind of "best-practice" security approach for NATO as a whole. Canadian and Dutch perspectives are also regularly present in the subject fields of Human Rights and International Law, Anthropology, and Literature / Linguistics.

Since 2005, the Academy has been in close collaboration with the Association for Canadian Studies in the Netherlands (ACSN). On the occasion of the 60th anniversary of the liberation, the Association organized a large conference, "Building Liberty: Canada and World Peace, 1945-2005", in cooperation with the Academy, and using its facilities in Middelburg. Since then my Canadian colleague at the Academy, Ernestine Lahey, has established the Canada Talks lecture series, with ACSN and Canadian Embassy support. Over the past two years, this multidisciplinary project has brought speakers on diverse topics such as Indigenous dialects, communication studies, and urban planning to give lectures in Middelburg. We look forward to further collaboration with ACSN to develop similar successful ventures.

I would like to conclude by thanking those I worked with in this book project. All five essayists have taken my classes in International Relations at some point over the past five years, and when this project was proposed, I knew whom I could ask to join me. The first chair of the Academy's Student Association was a Canadian – Jesse Coleman, author of the essay on Canada-EU relations in this book – and we have stayed in touch since he graduated in 2007. Moritz Baumgaertel and I worked together on a challenging International Relations project in 2009, resulting in a co-authored conference paper and publication. I greatly appreciated the input that Arlinda Rrustemi and Jacqueline Breidlid contributed to my classes, and this book has been a productive way to continue contact since they graduated. Djeyhoun Ostowar has been busy with a whole array of extra-curricular activities at the Academy, including organizing a top-level one-day event on Afghanistan in November last year. Their individual ability to produce an essay for this book, on top of their regular workload, has been exceptional. Finally, I would like to thank the editors, Conny Steenman Marcusse and Christl Verduyn, for successfully guiding this book to completion.

References

Ganzevoort, H. 1988. *A Bittersweet Land: The Dutch Experience in Canada*. Toronto: McClelland & Stewart.

Krieken, P. van. 2005. *The Hague: Legal Capital of the World*. Cambridge: Cambridge University Press.

OECD Statistics: http://stats.oecd.org/index.aspx

Statistics Canada (2006 census): http://www.statcan.gc.ca/

From "Dormant Giant" to "Enlightened Sovereignty":

Canadian and Dutch Contributions to the G20

Moritz Baumgaertel

As the number of global challenges grows, ties between Canada and the Netherlands have increased and strengthened. The ongoing financial crisis has moved one particular venue for international problem solving into the limelight. In 2008-2009, the Group of Twenty, or G20, changed from a forum that existed primarily on paper to a political body that increasingly determines the direction of the global economy and world finance. Agreements struck by state representatives at the meetings in Washington, London, and Pittsburgh have been remarkable not only in terms of their scope and significance but also in terms of their motives, which Canadian Prime Minister Stephen Harper has referred to as "enlightened sovereignty". Leaving behind the pursuit of relative gains in the power game of nations, "enlightened sovereignty" describes a more reasonable approach to international collaboration. Both the Netherlands and Canada have shown their adherence to this solid principle, albeit in distinct ways. The creation of the G20 a decade ago serves as a good starting point for an inquiry into its development.

Canada and the Creation of the Group of Twenty

The humble beginnings of the G20 date back to 1999, when the global economy was still recovering from two major crises: Mexico in 1994-95 and East Asia in 1997-98. These crises taught that the so-called "emerging markets" could no longer be ignored, due to their impact on the economies of the developed world. They showed that it was necessary to involve these states in the economic and financial decision making, which up till then had been undertaken mostly by the G7. There were obvious concerns that their inclusion would decrease the power of the developed countries. However, with the effects of the economic crises still fresh, various countries took the initiative to create deliberative forums where an open discussion on the global markets would be possible. The USA, under President Bill Clinton, hosted several informal gatherings for this purpose, such as the G22 (the Willard Group) and the G33. In spite of its leading position, the USA could not call such bodies into existence without the cooperation of others, and a consensus within the G7 was needed. As it happened, these countries wanted more than the USA.

Moritz Baumgaertel

Not satisfied with the outlook of the newly created forums, former Canadian Finance Minister Paul Martin took a leading role in bringing together the ideas of the USA, Germany, France, Italy, and Japan. In his view, there was a need to found a body where talk would be supplemented by action, with the declared aim being that "virtually no major aspect of the global economy or international financial system [would be] outside of the group's purview" (Beauchesne, 1999). Martin negotiated extensively with both developed and developing countries, and at the G7 conference in Cologne in 1999, the G20 was officially created. Due to the efforts of Martin and the Ministry of Finance, Canada became the first state to chair the G20.

The Group of Twenty had the mandate to "explore virtually every area of international finance and the potential to deal with some of the most visible and troubling aspects of today's integrated world economy – including the devastating effects of financial crises, the growing gap between rich and poor, and the system of governance that has not kept pace with the sweeping changes taking place in the global economy" (Martin, 2000). The beginnings of the G20 were undoubtedly ambitious. The Canadian vision offered a hint of the "enlightened sovereignty" that would fully develop nine years later.

Which countries became G20 members? Next to those of the G8 (Canada, France, Germany, Italy, Japan, Russia, the UK, and the USA), the forum encompassed a diverse set of countries, including Argentina, Australia, Brazil, China, India, Indonesia, Mexico, Saudi Arabia, South Africa, South Korea, and Turkey, as well as the European Union. One of the objectives of the forum was to cover a diversity of economic capacities around the world without impairing its ability to act. In contrast to the G7, the G20 sought to create a regional balance to bridge the North-South divide that had been one of the causes of the economic crises in 1994-95 and 1997-98. Based on these two points, the Netherlands was not initially a part of the planning of the G20. Ensuring an honest, open, and constructive dialogue between developed and developing states was the primary objective of the G20. One of the concessions was to not enlarge the forum with countries from the global North (the exception being Australia as an important regional participant). However, as the European Union became a permanent member of the G20, the Netherlands was still represented, if indirectly.

The G20 Takes Action: the 2008 Financial Crisis

After its establishment and following the initial attention it received, the G20 became a "dormant giant." Concerns other than economic and financial regulation dominated international politics: the 2001 attacks on the World Trade Center and the Pentagon, resulting in the War on Terror; the fight

©Embassy of India in Moscow

Group photo of the Heads of Delegations of the G-20 Summit at Pittsburgh, USA on 25 September 2009.

against the Taliban; and the invasion of Iraq. There was little attention to "enlightened sovereignty" or to a common strategy for fostering the global economy and regulating the financial sector. But the global financial crisis in 2008 brought the G20 back into focus. As the financial markets crashed and the fates of banks, companies, and millions of jobs hung in the balance, world leaders turned to Canada and to the G20 for solutions. The meeting of the G20 leaders in 2008 in Washington re-established media interest in the institution, bringing it back from the periphery to the centre of global financial regulation and international politics.

Without entering too far into the technicalities of the outcomes of the three G20 meetings that took place in Washington, London, and Pittsburgh, it is possible to note that a wide array of decisive measures was taken: raising capital requirements for financial institutions, installing macro-prudential supervision (the tracing of trends and systemic risks in the financial system), extending the scope of financial regulation, and reforming and strengthening the IMF – International Monetary Fund (Pisani-Ferry, Bénassy-Quéré, and Kumar, 2009). Canada's input into the discussion of appropriate policy measures has been considerable. Publications such as, amongst others, "Boring Canada's Financial Tips for the World" (Flaherty, 2008), present Canada's macro-economic and financial policy experience. As Canada's financial crisis was not as severe as others, particularly that of its southern neighbour, its advice was sought by many observers.

At the same time, the Netherlands became an important problem-solver in the G20. Although still not a permanent member, the Netherlands was invited because the country occupies 16th place in the IMF's 2008 GNP rankings, and it possesses the ninth largest financial sector, with large-scale insurance and pension interests. This made Dutch participation valuable. US President Barack Obama, hosting the Pittsburgh summit, also stressed the political weight of the Netherlands, its "very specific expertise and experience in working with a whole range of world leaders," and the fact that "the Prime Minister's contribution will be greatly appreciated" (The White House, 2009). This was reminiscent of the invitation to Prime Minister Wim Kok to attend the G8 in Denver in 1997 to explain the merits of Dutch economic policy.

How, then, has the Netherlands, invited only on an *ad hoc* basis by the respective G20 hosts, influenced these summits? One way has been to contribute as much as possible. According to Prime Minister Jan Peter Balkenende, the aim in 2009 was to establish a "stronger set of common values and principles guiding our economic activities," a clear reflection of the "enlightened sovereignty" approach of the forum. As the export-based economy of the Netherlands is greatly exposed to external influences, the Dutch have clear interests in enhancing the work of the G20. One illustrative example is the quick and constructive report that the Netherlands sent back to the Financial Stability Board following the meeting of the Finance Ministers at the G20 in St Andrews in 2009. Moreover, under the auspices of Bert Koenders, the Minister of Development Cooperation, the Dutch delegation presented a report in Pittsburgh on the position of the poorest countries in the global economy, considering issues such as adequate funds, development cooperation, and fair trade. The Netherlands has also supported increased voting rights for developing countries in international financial organizations, reflecting a more enlightened approach toward economics and finance. Like Canada, the Netherlands sees the general interest in overcoming the North-South divide. The support of the Netherlands for the G20 has therefore been considerable, regardless of the fact that it has not yet been ensured a permanent seat.

Looking Ahead: Future and Institutionalization of the G20

Ten years after the initial meeting of Finance Ministers and Central Bank Governors in Montreal, the G20 returns this year to its original host nation. The G20 summit in Toronto in June 2010 is in many ways extremely important for the Group, after Pittsburgh designated it as "the world's premier forum for economic cooperation" (Harper, 2010). First, exit strategies for the economic stimulus packages will be a focal point, as governments want to wind down their economic recovery programs. Second, one of the priorities of the Canadian organizers is the regulation of financial markets. According to Prime Minister Stephen Harper, it is time "to ensure transparency in the marketplace, help link risk, performance, and reward, and encourage a culture of prudent behaviour focused on the long term" (Harper, 2010). The Toronto summit might provide a turning point for establishing firmer and lasting regulations. Third, the Group's meeting in Canada is intended to foster global trade by reducing trade barriers. Speaking to the World Economic Forum in Davos in January 2010, Prime Minister Harper stressed that protectionist measures will only prolong the financial crisis. Since Canada also chairs the G8 meetings this year, the country will occupy a key role as mediator between the two forums. The realization of economic and political projects this year will depend on Canada's success in convincing the world's leaders of the continued importance of "enlightened sovereignty" – a task that the Canadian hosts are well aware of.

At the same time, 2010 will also reveal the institutional direction of the G20. The crisis years have given the forum increasing importance on issues of finance and economics in the eyes of both policy-makers and the public. However, it faces serious competition from alternative global institutions. There is much talk of a G2, encompassing only the USA and China, or a G3, which would make the European Union the third pillar in a new global order. The argument for such power conglomerates is clear: without the initiative of the major economic powers, policy changes cannot be enforced, be it in economics, security, or exclusively global issues such as climate change. However, such notions seem short-sighted as they overlook the reason for the emergence of the G20. Negotiating global challenges – and particularly the outlook of the world economy – needs to involve a wide range of participants. No single country can control the web of complex interdependence that links financial sectors and economies. "Enlightened sovereignty", as promoted by Canada and the Netherlands, takes into account the specific nature of contemporary political, economic, and social problems. The G20 is therefore here to stay as a forum in which developed states and emerging market economies will be able to decide measures that make a true difference on a global scale.

The G20's role will also continue to raise questions about participation and membership. As an "in-between" state, the Netherlands has sought to make a case for a permanent seat. The Dutch claim legitimacy based not only on their important place in world finance but also on their constructive contributions. The strategy seems to be successful so far, reflected for instance, in the US President Obama's promise to Crown Prince Willem-Alexander in September 2009 to involve the Dutch in the G20 on a long-term basis. Securing a permanent place, however, will not be easy. The primary concern of the Netherlands is therefore to ensure the continuation of *ad hoc* invitations which, based on its participation in the last three meetings, are slowly becoming established. Such an approach reflects a willingness to foster global development rather than one's own prestige, an attitude which, in the aftermath of the financial crisis, seems appropriate. As Stephen Harper remarked in early 2010: "it doesn't matter what global structures we devise for our mutual betterment, if we don't have the right global attitudes, they will not work" (Harper, 2010). In this sense, both Canada and the Netherlands are global leaders, one step ahead of those that have not yet fully understood the meaning of international collaboration in the 21st century.

References

Balkenende, Jan Peter. 2009. "London the starting point for a new global consensus." Retrieved from http://www.londonsummit.gov.uk/en/global-update/cp-netherlands/jan-peter-balkenende

Beauchesne, Eric. 1999. "Martin warns against complacency." *Montreal Gazette*. 26 September 1999: A9.

Flaherty, James. 2008. "Boring Canada's financial tips for the world." *Financial Times*, 12 November 2008: A13.

Harper, Stephen. 2010. "Recovery and New Beginnings." Davos, 28 January 2010. Retrieved from http://pm.gc.ca/eng/media.asp?id=3101

Martin, Paul. 2000. Speech to the House of Commons Standing Committee on Foreign Affairs and International Trade. Ottawa, 18 May 2010. Retrieved from http://www.collectionscanada.gc.ca/webarchives/20071122053134/http://www.fin.gc.ca/news00/00-041e.html

Pisani-Ferry, Jean, Agnès Bénassy-Quéré and Rajiv Kumar. 2009. "The G20 is not just a G7 with extra chairs," *Bruegel Policy Contributions*, September 2009. Retrieved from http://www.bruegel.org/uploads/tx_btbbreugel/pc_G20_not_G7_061009.pdf

The White House. 2009. Remarks by President Obama and Prime Minister Balkenende of the Netherlands after Meeting. Washington, D.C. 14 July 2009. Retrieved from http://www.whitehouse.gov/the_press_office/Remarks-by-President-Obama-and-Prime-Minister-Balkenende-of-the-Netherlands-after-meeting

Copenhagen and After: Coping with Climate Change

Jacqueline Breidlid

Since the 1980s, there have been increasing concerns and rising global awareness about the critical impact of global climate change. This has led to the establishment of the UN Climate Change Panel, and to the first global response efforts in the 1990s with the adoption of the UN Framework Treaty and the Kyoto Protocol. Both Canada and the Netherlands have become signatories of these treaties and have recently aligned themselves with the 2009 Copenhagen Accord, by which they agree to non-binding emissions reductions as of 2012. This essay presents an overview of the different threats and challenges that the Netherlands and Canada face when it comes to climate change, as well as a perspective on their political cooperation strategy. It also considers potential areas for cooperation or possibilities for learning from each other's experiences in dealing with climate change.

Different Threats and Challenges

While climate change is a concern for all countries, the fact that Canada and the Netherlands have quite unique geographies and demographic compositions means that it poses distinct challenges to each of them.

With its enormous land mass and vast wilderness areas, and with part of its territory within the Arctic Circle, Canada faces special concerns about change in global temperatures. Melting ice caps have a direct influence on the natural environment of northern Canada. This is particularly dramatic for animal and plant species that are vulnerable to a quickly changing environment. There are also repercussions for northern Canadian Indigenous communities whose traditional life styles are being threatened (Arctic Council and IASC, 2004). On the other hand, ice cap melt in the Arctic region is opening new trading routes for vessels and new opportunities for exploration and exploitation of natural resources. Developing a legal system to ensure that the increasingly accessible Arctic Ocean will receive enough environmental protection is a challenge ahead for Canada and other Arctic nations (Ho, 2010).

At the same time, Canada has a growing population and is dependent on its economically significant energy sector and its natural resources. Tar sands (oil mixed with sand and clay) represent a resource of strategic importance to North America; however, the extraction process requires a disproportionate amount of energy (Pembina Institute, 2005 and Raitt, 2009).

Jacqueline Breidlid

In contrast to Canada, the Netherlands is relatively small in size and is densely populated. The most direct threat posed by climate change involves the fact that a quarter of the country lies below sea level (minlnv.nl, 2009). Rising sea levels could therefore have devastating effects, a possibility that technology cannot necessarily solve. As Prime Minister Jan Peter Balkenende reminded listeners in his statement to the Copenhagen summit, the Netherlands was forced to take urgent measures after a destructive flood in 1953 to prevent such a disaster from happening again. A similar sense of urgency is now needed in response to the threat of climate change. As nearly half the land mass is used for farming (minlnv.nl, 2008), the agricultural sector is especially vulnerable to such threats (de Groot et. al., 2006). An ongoing challenge for the Netherlands is that of combining the expanding economic and leisure activities while at the same time attaining sustainable development (vrom.nl).

National Policies and the Kyoto Protocol

Canada has planned to reduce greenhouse gas emissions on a national level through a focus on green investments and clean energy research. Additionally, it has introduced draft rules for the "Turning the Corner" Initiative, which will require its industry to reduce GHG emissions through strict regulatory standards, and which envisages the establishment of an emissions trading market as well as a market price for carbon (climatechange.gc.ca).

The Netherlands' climate change policy is deeply embedded within the environmental policy of the European Union, whose decisions and directives are binding. EU leaders endorsed an integrated approach to climate change and energy policy in 2007 and made a unilateral commitment that Europe would cut its emissions by at least 20% of 1990 levels by 2020. This goal is to be implemented in each of the member-states through a package of binding legislation that sets up the European Union Emissions Trading System (EU ETS), a system of effort-sharing in sectors not covered by the EU ETS, binding national targets for renewable energy and a legal framework for Carbon Capture and Storage (CCS). The Netherlands aims to implement the obligations set by the EU through the "Clean and Efficient: New Energy for Climate Policy", the goals of which are to reduce GHG emissions by 30% from 1990 levels, to double the rate of energy efficiency, and to reach a high share of renewable energy (vrom.nl).

Canada and the Netherlands both made early commitments to climate change on the global level by signing the Kyoto Protocol. While the Netherlands has generally been successful in complying with the assigned emissions reductions (Europa, 2009), reports indicate that Canada will have difficulties in meeting the targets until the expiration of the Kyoto Protocol in 2012 (see, for example, Greenpeace, 2010). A specific challenge that Canada faces on the local level is the coordination of climate policy at the federal and provincial levels, since provinces have their own, often quite diverse, environmental policies (Report on 2005 Dutch-Canadian Conference, 42). Another difficulty for Canada is its strong economic integration with the USA, which has so far not signed the Kyoto Protocol. Canadian focus on climate change seems to have shifted from Kyoto towards new post-2012 commitments (Environment Canada, 2009).

Political Cooperation on Climate Change

Although the two countries are differently threatened by climate change, Canada and the Netherlands maintain a constructive political dialogue on the problem. Cooperation between Canada and the EU on environmental issues began in the 1970s, with the exchange of letters of intent on environmental cooperation. A high-level Canada-EU dialogue on environment now takes place every 18 months to compare environmental policy and progress. Additionally there is an annual Canada-EU summit, with the environment regularly on the agenda. The 2007 summit resulted in a specific commitment to work together to combat climate change and an agreement to establish a Canada-EU dialogue on energy (canadainternational.gc.ca).

Bilateral relations have also produced results. In 2005, Canada and the Netherlands held a multi-stakeholder conference in Ottawa entitled "Innovation in Combating Climate Change". The conference brought together experts from government, the private sector, and civil society to address specific challenges related to national responses to climate policy, to development and use of economic and market-based mechanisms, and specifically to technological innovation for combating climate change (Conference Report, 2005). Key areas for potential cooperation were the exchange of information in technological sectors such as Carbon Capture and Storage, and the future linking of emissions trading schemes. Canada and the Netherlands have also met each other in global frameworks such as the recent Climate Change summit in Copenhagen. Their official positions were quite similar. Both emphasized that developed countries should take ambitious action, but that developing countries also should respond, and share the burden according to their capabilities and responsibilities. The two countries also agreed to back an international fund to support this process, and to increase the development of clean technologies such as Carbon Capture and Storage. The main divergence between the Dutch and Canadian positions was that Canada further emphasized that environmental protection needs to be balanced with economic prosperity to avoid any undue burden on growth (see climatechange.gc.ca and vrom.nl respectively).

The outcome of the negotiations was that Canada oriented itself around the US commitment to reduce carbon-based emissions by 17% below 2005 levels, and the Netherlands committed itself to the EU target of 20% below

Courtesy Algkalv.

The melting of ice-caps makes the arctic environment particularly vulnerable to climate change.

1990 levels (or 30% if other countries follow). The Accord also provided for additional financing for developing countries between 2010-2012, and established the Copenhagen Green Climate Fund to help poorer countries adapt to and mitigate the effects of climate change (Environment Canada Media Lines, 2010).

Canada and the Netherlands share similar concerns and approaches in the area of technological innovation and the development of market mechanisms. Three issues for discussion here include agricultural greenhouse gases, carbon capture and storage, and emissions trading.

1. Agricultural Greenhouse Gases

Agriculture is estimated to be responsible for about 14% of global human-induced greenhouse gas emissions (FAO, 2009), a relatively high amount that has only recently received more attention. The main greenhouse gases emitted are methane from livestock digestion and manure, and nitrous oxide resulting from manure handling and storage and from commercial fertilizers (minlnv.nl). During the Copenhagen summit, both the Netherlands and Canada showed their willingness to tackle this issue by becoming founding members of the "Alliance on Agricultural Greenhouse Gas Emissions", which aims to research and to prevent GHG emissions from farming (cordis.lu).

The agricultural sector in Canada is estimated to be responsible for 8.6% of total national GHG emissions and has been a significant contributor to the overall growth in emissions since 1990 (National Greenhouse Gas Inventory 1990-2006, 2008). When Canada became part of the Global Alliance,

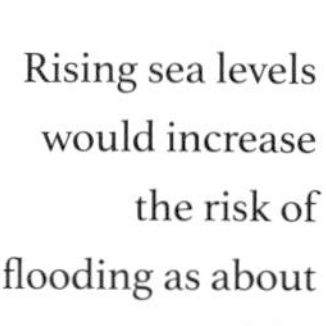

Rising sea levels would increase the risk of flooding as about a quarter of the Dutch land lies below sea level.

Courtesy Stadsweb

Environment Minister Jim Prentice emphasized that "by developing new ways to reduce the GHG emissions from agricultural activities, this Government is working to help Canadian farmers to continue to show leadership and share their best practices. Scientists around the world are working to find new ways to reduce emissions and decrease poverty and this alliance will serve to identify gaps in existing research and increase international collaboration" (www.ec.gc.ca). Canada will invest up to $27 million in the Global Research Alliance, dedicated to working towards solutions in this sector.

Despite its relatively small size, the Netherlands is among the world's three largest exporters of agricultural products, and the agri-complex share in the economy is nearly 10% (Ministry of Agriculture, Nature and Food Quality, 2008). The agricultural sector clearly plays an important role in climate change, not only because it is a sector that emits greenhouse gases (in 2007 about 25Mt out of the 207Mt total), but also because it is one of the sectors that is most vulnerable to climate change, especially to the risk of flooding (see de Groot et. al., 2006, and Netherlands National Inventory Report, 2008). The Netherlands is taking an innovative approach to this problem by focusing on the development of precision farming and alternative feedstock for cattle (*Convenant Schone en Zuinige Agrosektoren*). It is also planning to introduce a national emissions trading system specifically for the agricultural sector, where emitters can trade their emissions rights with each other (minlnv.nl, Jaarplan 2010).

2. Technology Innovation – a Common Focus on Carbon Capture and Storage

One of the findings of the 2005 Dutch-Canadian Conference on Climate Change was that climate-friendly technologies require increasing investment in research and economic incentives to put the technologies to use (2005

Conference Report, 19). Technological innovation for both countries seems to be particularly promising in the field of Carbon Capture and Storage (CCS), a technique that allows carbon to be stored under the ground instead of being released into the atmosphere.

The rationale behind this technique is that, while technologies are being developed to take advantage of alternative energy resources (solar, wind, biomass), "most scenarios project that the supply of primary energy will continue to be dominated by fossil fuels until at least the middle of the century" (IPCC, 2005, 3). CCS is a means to continue using fossil fuels in a climate-friendly manner by capturing the released carbon dioxide and storing it in specially selected geological formations underground (Meerman et. al., 2008). In 2009, both Canada and the Netherlands became founding members of the newly launched Global Capture and Storage Institute, which will help accelerate the deployment of CCS demonstration projects worldwide (www.globalccsinstitute.com).

It is estimated that Canada could store about three-quarters of its current greenhouse gas emissions underground, and geological formations in western Canada are considered ideal for CO2 storage (Pembina Institute, 2005). One of the world's first full-scale demonstrations of CCS will take place at a coal-fired electricity plant in Saskatchewan (www.pm.gc.ca), and other projects have been announced in Alberta (Environment Canada Media Lines, 2010).

The Netherlands takes the position that, although it aims to achieve a 100% sustainable energy system, CCS offers a solution for the transition from fossil fuels to sustainable sources of energy (vrom.nl). It has a potential storage capacity in depleted gas or oil fields, and much of the technical knowledge required for this solution is already present (vrom.nl). The Dutch government and the EU support CCS research, and finance both small and large-scale demonstration projects, the first of which will be launched in 2015 (www.co2-cato.nl). An indicator of Dutch leadership in this field is that two of the three EU pilot projects are coordinated by Dutch research institutes (Meerman et. al., 2008).

Cooperation in developing CCS as a transition technique (until there is less reliance on fossil fuels) is in the interest of both states. The technology will contribute to meeting the commitments each has set under the Copenhagen Accord, and could potentially be implemented into future emissions trading systems.

3. Emissions Trading – Market Mechanisms as the Way Forward?

Under the Kyoto Protocol (Art. 17), parties with commitments to reduce their greenhouse gas emissions have the opportunity to engage in trading their assigned amounts. A country that does not manage to reach its reduction targets can, in other words, buy the excess capacity of other countries on the international "carbon market" (www.unfccc.int).

The European Union has already established the so-called EU Emissions Trading Scheme (ETS). A European Directive requires member-states such as the Netherlands to set up a Cap and Trade System and a National Allocation Plan, which stipulate the exact emissions allocated to each company. Members of the EU are now in the second trading period (2008-2012) and a third period will take place between 2013 and 2020. While only a limited number of sectors was included in the first and second trading periods, the third trading period envisages the inclusion of new sectors such as aviation. New technologies such as CCS will be taken into account, meaning that stored CO2 could be subtracted from CO2 emissions (www.ec.europa.eu).

Although North America has not introduced a regional Cap and Trade System, there is potential for similar arrangements between Canadian provinces or in collaboration with the USA and/or with Mexico. Some Canadian provinces and American states have already collaborated to create carbon markets between them. One example is the Western Climate Initiative involving six western American states and four Canadian provinces (www.westernclimateinitiative.org). The first phase of this collaboration is scheduled to begin in January 2012, matching the first commitment period of the Copenhagen Accord.

During the Copenhagen summit, Canada reaffirmed its commitment to work with provincial and territorial governments and its partners to develop and implement a North American Cap and Trade System for greenhouse gas emissions (Environment Canada Media Lines, 2010). Additionally, the 2005 Dutch-Canadian conference on Climate Change resulted in a commitment to further explore linking emissions trading schemes and to step up bilateral cooperation (Conference Report, 2005).

One advantage for Canada in the existing Cap and Trade System in Europe is that lessons can be learned from the obstacles the system has encountered. For instance, in the first and second trading periods of the ETS, most emitters were allocated their emissions rights free of charge, under a system called "grandfathering" (Scott, 2009). In addition, during the first trial period (2005-2007), emitters were actually often allocated more emission rights than they needed, due to difficulties in predicting "business as usual" emissions (Ellerman, Joskow, 2008). If Canada were to implement a similar system it could consider how over-allocation might be avoided and whether emissions rights should be auctioned off immediately. Likewise, the EU example has revealed that the goal of significantly reducing emissions can only be achieved by tightening mandatory caps on permissible emissions, so that these become scarcer and more valuable, thereby providing incentives for businesses to introduce their own tighter controls, something which Canada might be prepared to do better. Another source of inspiration is the current debate in the EU whether the auction revenues should be used to fund climate change protection within the EU or in developing countries (Euractiv, 2008 and EC Environment, 2010).

Both Canada and the Netherlands stand to gain if Canada were to establish a Cap and Trade System, as, in the end, a carbon market will work most effectively if it is at the global level and includes as many emitters as possible.

The Way Forward after Copenhagen

Canada and the Netherlands (through the EU) remain committed to continuing negotiations towards implementing a new, legally binding agreement when the Kyoto Protocol expires. The Copenhagen Accord paved the way by including all major emitters, and by setting quantifiable emissions reductions levels. Future Canadian climate policy will depend heavily on the direction taken by US policy and the chances of a US climate bill. The two economies are so closely integrated that it makes little sense to proceed without harmonizing and aligning climate policy principles, policies, regulations, and standards (Environment Canada Media Lines, 2010).

The European Commission will soon announce its 2020 strategy towards "enabling the EU to make a full recovery from the crisis, while speeding up the move towards a smart and green technology" (http://ec.europa.eu/eu2020/). While states need to work together on a global scale in order to create a new binding treaty, strong bilateral cooperation in climate change can lay the basis for wider agreement. For Canada and the Netherlands, exchanging innovative technologies and learning from each other's experiences is the immediate way forward.

References

Official government websites

Canadian government website entitled "Office of the Prime Minister" at www.pm.gc.ca/eng

Canadian government website entitled "Canada's Action on Climate Change", at http://www.climatechange.gc.ca/

Dutch Ministry of Housing, Spatial Planning and the Environment. 2009. United Nations Conference in Copenhagen at http://international.vrom.nl/pagina.html?id=45605

Dutch Ministry of Agriculture, Nature and Food Quality (minlnv) at www.minlnv.nl

European Commission website on Climate Change at http://ec.europa.eu/environment/climat/home_en.htm

European Commission website on the Emissions Trading Scheme at http://ec.europa.eu/environment/climat/emission/index_en.htm

Media reports and articles

Dutch Ministry of Agriculture, Nature and Food Quality. 2008. "Facts and Figures 2008 of the Dutch Agri-Sector." Retrieved from www.minlnv.nl

Dutch Ministry of Agriculture, Nature and Food Quality, *Convenant Schone en Zuinige Agrosectoren,* retrieved from minlnv.nl

Dutch Ministry of Agriculture, Nature and Food Quality, *Programma Kas als Energiebron, Jaarplan 2010:* 6.

Dutch-Canadian Conference on Climate Change. 2005. Conference Report "Innovation in Combating Climate Change." Ottawa, 6-7 October 2005.

EC Environment. 2010. "Emissions Trading System." Retrieved from http://ec.europa.eu/environment/climat/emission/auctioning_en.htm

Environment Canada. 2009. A Climate Change Plan for the Purpose of the Kyoto Protocol Implementation Act 2009. Retrieved from http://www.ec.gc.ca/doc/ed-es/KPIA2009/s1_eng.htm

Environment Canada Media Lines. 2010. *Canada on Climate Change*, COMM 2010-0037 CC. 26 January 2010.

Euractiv. 2008. "EU Emissions Trading Scheme: 'Use permit revenues to fund climate change protection,' says Environment Committee." Retrieved from http://pr.euractiv.com/node/6052

Europa. 2009. "Climate Change: Progress report shows EU on track to meet or over-achieve Kyoto emissions target." Retrieved from http://europa.eu/rapid/pressReleasesAction.do?reference=IP/09/1703&format=HTML&aged=0&language=EN&guiLanguage=en

Greenpeace. 2010. "Canada and Kyoto." Retrieved February 2010 from http://www.greenpeace.org/canada/en/campaigns/kyotoplus/background/canada-and-kyoto

News Release. "Canada Becomes Founding Member of the Global Research Alliance on Agricultural Greenhouse Gases." Retrieved from www.ec.gc.ca

Raitt, Lisa. 2009. Notes for a speech by the Honourable Lisa Raitt, P.C., M.P., Minister of Natural Resources to Canada's Oil Sands: "A Strategic Resource for North America." Retrieved November 2009 from Natural Resources Canada website at http://www.nrcan-rncan.gc.ca/media/spedis/2009/2009114-eng.php

The Canadian Cattlemen's Association. "GHG Factsheets: Agriculture and greenhouse gases." Retrieved from www.cattle.ca

Academic and Scientific Reports

Arctic Council and International Arctic Science Committee. 2004. "Arctic Climate Impact Assessment," issued by fourth Arctic Council Ministerial Meeting. Reykjavik, 24 November 2004. Retrieved from http://www.acia.uaf.edu/

Groot, R.S. de, et. al. 2006. "Climate Change Scientific Assessment and Policy Analysis, Climate adaptation in the Netherlands." Retrieved from Netherlands National Institute for Public Health and the Environment website http://www.rivm.nl/en/

Ellerman, A.D., Joskow, P.L. 2008. "The European Union's Emissions Trading System in Perspective," prepared for the Pew Center on Global Climate Change. Massachusetts's Institute of Technology. Retrieved from http://www.pewclimate.org/docUploads/EU-ETS-In-Perspective-Report.pdf

Food and Agriculture Organisation (FAO). 2009. "Agriculture is essential for facing Climate Change." Retrieved February 2010 from http://www.fao.org/news/story/en/item/20243/icode/

Ho, J. 2010. "The implications of Arctic sea ice decline on shipping." Marine policy, 34:3.

Meerman, J.C., Kuramochi, T., Egmond, S. 2008. "CO2 Capture Research in the Netherlands." Retrieved from www.co2-cato.nl

National Inventory Report 1990-2005. 2008. The Canadian Government's Submission to the UN Framework Convention on Climate Change. May. Retrieved from http://www.ec.gc.ca/pdb/ghg/inventory_report/2005_report/2005_report_e.pdf

National Inventory Report 2008, *Greenhouse Gas Emissions in the Netherlands 1990-2006*, retrieved from http://www.rivm.nl/bibliotheek/rapporten/500080009.pdf

Scott, M. 2009. "Avoiding Europe's Carbon Trading Missteps". Business week online, 0:10.

The Pembina Institute. 2005. "Carbon Capture and Storage: An arrow in the quiver or a silver bullet to combat climate change? A Canadian Primer." Research conducted by Griffiths, Cobb, Marr-Laing.

The Pembina Institute. 2005. "Oil Sans Fever: The Environmental Implications of Canada's Oil Sands Rush." Wollnillowicz, D., Baker, C.S., Raynolds, M. November.

Working Group III of the Intergovernmental Panel on Climate Change. 2005. IPCC Special Report on Carbon Dioxide Capture and Storage. New York: Cambridge University Press. Retrieved 2010 from http://www1.ipcc.ch/ipccreports/srccs.htm

Canada's Ongoing Relationship with Europe: a Brief History since Word War II

Jesse Coleman

Canada's relationship with the European Union has developed through a growing interest in trade relations, especially as Canada has looked to expand its horizons away from reliance on the United States. Trade is an important issue for Canada, which has a wealth of natural resources. Europe offers a lucrative market for these and other resources. This essay will highlight how trade across the Atlantic Ocean between Canada and the EU has developed and evolved since the 19th century.

Background

The European origin of a majority of Canadian immigrants before the second half of the 20th century has played a key role in Canada's perception of Europe. Canada's late 19th and early 20th century international relations dealt largely with the United States, due to proximity, and with Britain, due to ancestry. Interaction with continental Europe was comparatively limited until World War I, when Canada became involved in the war through its ties with Britain. Even after more than 67,000 Canadians died during the Great War of 1914-1918, relations with continental Europe remained relatively limited.

During the inter-war years, Canada's place on the international stage was not among the most prominent, even though it was a full and founding member of the League of Nations, which could have been the basis for a greater level of interaction with European countries. The Canadian government of the day was not particularly interested in international relations beyond those with the United States, and most effort was directed towards gaining further independence from Britain. The Great Depression affected Canada significantly and contributed to a certain degree of further isolation from the international scene. When Hitler invaded Poland on 1 September 1939, however, Canadian Prime Minister Mackenzie King's immediate reaction was that Canada should lend military support to defeat Germany. Parliament debated the matter quickly and declared war. Nearly 10% of the Canadian population served during World War II, and Canadians were instrumental in helping to liberate Western Europe. Over 45,000 Canadians died and many more were wounded. Following the war, thousands of Europeans immigrated to Canada in search of a different life.

Jesse Coleman

Dealing with a Uniting Europe

As an original signatory of the North Atlantic Treaty, which brought NATO into existence on 4 April 1949, Canada showed the world that World War II had effectively ended its isolationism. Relations with Europe, however, would be influenced by ongoing processes of economic and political integration. The creation of the European Coal and Steel Community (ECSC) in 1950 heralded a new era and introduced an extra layer of complexity to the field of international relations. Canada did not initially see the ECSC as a threat since its largest European trading partner, Britain, was not a member.

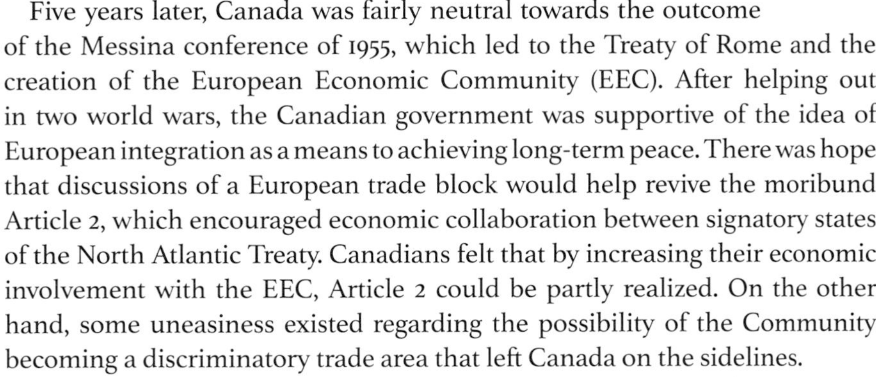

Five years later, Canada was fairly neutral towards the outcome of the Messina conference of 1955, which led to the Treaty of Rome and the creation of the European Economic Community (EEC). After helping out in two world wars, the Canadian government was supportive of the idea of European integration as a means to achieving long-term peace. There was hope that discussions of a European trade block would help revive the moribund Article 2, which encouraged economic collaboration between signatory states of the North Atlantic Treaty. Canadians felt that by increasing their economic involvement with the EEC, Article 2 could be partly realized. On the other hand, some uneasiness existed regarding the possibility of the Community becoming a discriminatory trade area that left Canada on the sidelines.

When the EEC emerged in 1957, it fuelled further Canadian concern about the consequences of British membership. Britain was still one of Canada's largest trading partners, and its membership in the EEC would mean preferential trading partnerships with other member-states, at Canada's expense. Considering the support that Canada had contributed just over a decade earlier in World War II, there was a sense of betrayal and disappointment among Canadians. Fortunately for Canada's trade balance, British membership of the EEC would not occur for another 15 years.

In order to avoid exclusion from the EEC, Canada worked to find a way for Canadian firms to penetrate the newly created market. After two years of hard work, in 1959, Canada struck an official relationship with the EEC through a minor trade agreement signed with the ECSC. The same year, Canada's ambassador to Belgium was given accreditation by the EEC. These events, however small, were seen as a signal of Canada's willingness to develop a healthy trade relationship with Europe. Nevertheless, Canada's trade relations with Europe as a whole were in relative decline while its trade relations with the United States continued to grow steadily.

Trudeau and Europe

Pierre Trudeau, who served as Canada's Prime Minister for 15 years, was a defining figure in the country's history. First elected in 1969, his government practised "quasi-isolationalism ... in the early years" (Granatstein and

A child leans over to smell a tulip at the Canadian Tulip Festival in Ottawa, Canada. The festival is held every spring in honour of the gift of tulip bulbs from the Netherlands.

Courtesy Marie-Marthe Gagnon.

Bothwell, 1990: 158). It took the introduction of tariffs on Canadian goods and the floating of the American dollar by President Richard Nixon in August 1971 to force Trudeau's government to adopt a more nuanced position on international relations and trade.

Changes in American trade policy were a sign to Canada that any "special relationship" it had with the USA was not as strong as may have been thought, and that Washington was willing to act in ways contrary to its northern ally's interests. In response, the Canadian government aimed to mitigate its economic dependence on the USA by focusing on relations beyond North America. In late 1971, Trudeau's government commissioned a wide-ranging study to look at Canada's options in the rest of the world. Despite this new global outlook, by 1972 Trudeau had still not visited Western Europe, although he affirmed that his support for NATO was solid.

The crucial breakthrough for Canadian international relations came in 1972 when Mitchell Sharp, former Secretary of State for External Affairs, proposed three options for Canada:

a) maintain more or less its present relationship with the United States with a minimum of policy adjustments;
b) move deliberately towards closer integration with the United States;
c) pursue a comprehensive long-term strategy to develop and strengthen the Canadian economy and other aspects of national life and in the process reduce Canada's trade vulnerability (Sharp, 1972: 106-107).

While the second option received no support from Sharp's colleagues, the first option was the choice of both the trade and the finance departments. Conversely, a majority of the government's cabinet, along with the Prime Minister, supported the third option. Although it was riskier, the third option was seen as more sensible in the long term. This meant searching out closer contacts elsewhere, including with the EEC.

In mid-1972, Canadian trade officials travelled to Brussels with a proposal. They suggested that Canada and the EEC sign an agreement to allow Canada "most-favoured-nation" status within the European Community. Such an agreement would ensure that no third country would receive more favourable access to the European market for its goods and services than Canada would. With initial negotiations moving slowly, Trudeau visited Europe in 1974, and again in 1975, to help matters along. The Canadian press derided Trudeau's first trip to Europe as a case of "scrambling" to put together a "headline-grabbing trade accord" (Granatstein and Bothwell, 1990: 166). Meetings with the Europeans did not fare much better, with one senior French official telling Trudeau: "Don't be more European than the Europeans .... You're ahead of us. You want more than we have reached" (ibid).

Trudeau's second visit to Europe was more successful. During a statement in London, he outlined Canada's goal of a contractual link with the Community. This would establish an open dialogue between Canada and Europe and ensure communication throughout the various phases and developments the EEC might experience in the future. Trudeau knew that the idea of a European Community was evolving, and he saw opportunities for Canada in this process. As he told Harold Wilson, the British Prime Minister at the time, "our policy of diversification is not anti-American. It was designed to reduce dependency on the United States by supplementing rather than supplanting relations with that country" (Granatstein and Bothwell, 1990: 167-168). Trudeau saw increasing contact with Europe as a means to achieve the third option that Sharp had proposed in 1972.

After years of bargaining, on 1 October 1976, the Framework Agreement on Commercial and Economic Cooperation came into effect. This was the first such accord that the EEC (now known as the European Community or EC) had with a third country, "other than with those that were connected to [Europe] by colonial history, as in Africa, or, indeed, in the Mediterranean" (Beck, 1996: 77). The final text of the agreement gave "most-favoured-nation" status to Canada in the EC and vice-versa, provided a framework to promote commercial cooperation, and called for the facilitation and encouragement of investment, joint ventures, and the exchange of scientists and information. The agreement was to remain in effect indefinitely, and could not be terminated before five years from the day of accord. The framework also ensured EC members the ability to make additional bilateral agreements with Canada.

The framework, however, did not prove to be the success that Trudeau had hoped. In the end, it was limited in scope and left much to be desired by those looking for a breakthrough in relations with Europe. Signing a treaty was one thing, but getting industry to take advantage of the opportunities offered was another. There was trepidation on both sides of the Atlantic as Canadian bankers and businessmen had little or no experience with the European market, let alone the linguistic abilities to interact in German, Dutch, or French, just to mention a few of the languages of Europe. The Europeans, for the most part, ignored investing in Canada due to its much smaller market (compared to the USA) and questioned small Canadian firms' ability to supply their large markets. A weak global economy in the 1970s, undermined by two energy crises, also negatively affected trade between Canada and Europe. Ultimately, however, the framework failed due to a lack of political will on the part of the Canadian government to insist on its provisions.

The 1980s and 1990s – Europe, the Fisheries Dispute and NAFTA

Following the defeat of Trudeau's Liberal government and the election of Brian Mulroney and his Progressive Conservative Party in 1985, a Royal Commission, which had been struck under Trudeau's government, reported on the state of the economy. The Commission recommended free trade with the United States, and despite the fact that the Commission was headed up by a member of the opposition, Mulroney embraced its findings. This marked a major departure from Sharp's third option for expanding Canada's international trade relations, on which Trudeau and his cabinet had spent so much time and effort.

The immediate result of this shift was Canadian trade reorientation towards the United States. From this came both the Free Trade Agreement (FTA) in 1988 and the North American Free Trade Agreement (NAFTA) in 1994, each introduced by Mulroney. These agreements had more breadth and depth than the earlier arrangement with Europe, and they led to increased levels of trade between the signatories. Contributing to the success of the FTA and NAFTA was Europe's own inward focus at the time. The creation of the Single European Act of 1985 and the Maastricht Treaty of 1991 left many nation states outside Europe unsure about how to move forward. Meanwhile, trade and communication among NAFTA countries grew, further diverting attention and focus away from Europe.

Trade contact between Canada and Europe during the 1980s dwindled to a minimum. Nevertheless, as the decade wore on and the outcome of European integration and the formation of the European Union (EU) were understood, Canada-EC relations shifted "from a condition of benign neglect to a search for new and substantive policy responses in both the economic and political

AP Photo

Canadian troops in landing craft approach a stretch of coastline code-named Juno Beach, near Bernières-sur-Mer, as the Allied Normandy invasion gets under way, on 6 June 1944.

spheres" (Potter, 1999:70). In 1990, political ties were strengthened through the EC-Canada Transatlantic Declaration. This agreement focused on opening doors to discussions between the two parties, including regular meetings of the Canadian Prime Minister and the President of the European Council, as well as between various trade-related officials on both sides.

In 1994, a Canada-EU conference was held in Toronto to discuss the status of their relationship. The main question, as posed in the keynote address by the Canadian Minister for International Trade, Roy MacLaren, was: "How do we revitalize the transatlantic community?" (Christensen, 1994: 8). The concept of the "transatlantic community" opened up discussions to include the United States, most likely as a result of the NAFTA negotiations.

Once again, the 1994 Canada-EU conference did not produce a major leap forward; indeed, it was followed a year later by a major dispute over fishing rights. The dispute started in 1994 when Canada observed more than 200 non-Canadian fishing boats crossing into the coastal 200-nautical mile Exclusive Economic Zone, off its eastern shores. In a bid to protect Canada's vulnerable fish stocks, the Federal Minister of Fisheries and Oceans, Brian Tobin, launched an aggressive dialogue with the European Union over the presence of European fishing trawlers in Canadian waters and over the equipment the trawlers were using, which was harming fish habitats.

In March 1996, with tensions still high, Canada decided to make an example of the Spanish fishing trawler, *Estai*. A Canadian Fisheries Patrol vessel chased and fired at the trawler before detaining it for several weeks. The Canadian government even held an international press conference outside the UN building in New York, reproaching the Spanish and EU governments for allowing the use of an environmentally-unsound fishing net. The incident soured Canada-EU relations, and communication between Ottawa and Brussels was muted for a number of years afterwards.

Recent Rumblings

Throughout the expansion of the EU, the Canadian government has for the most part refrained from public comment on the organization. This is not to say that Canada has stayed completely out of the picture, since, as a federal nation, there has been plenty of interest in the developing governance structure of the EU. But Canada has focused most of its attention on trade-related issues.

Since the 1990s, Canada has fallen from the list of the EU's top ten trading partners, to 11th place, where it has remained for a number of years. In an attempt to prevent further fall, a bilateral framework between the government of Canada and the European Commission was negotiated in 2004. This Framework on Regulatory Cooperation and Transparency is non-binding and covers four main areas of relations: regulatory governance, regulatory practice, facilitation of trade and investment, and competitiveness and innovation. The framework emerged out of the March 2004 EU-Canada summit and brought both parties closer together after years of strained relations in the wake of the fisheries conflict.

The 2007 EU-Canada summit statement led to another commitment from both parties to continue fostering their relationship. The statement highlighted the three focus areas of the summit itself: peace and security, economic partnerships, and energy and climate change. The rationale for each is apparent. Both Canada and the EU are investing in improving the security of their territories, and both have contributed military support in the ongoing Afghanistan conflict. With respect to economic partnerships, the EU is Canada's second largest trading partner. Finally, for the EU and Canada alike, the environment and energy are highly important issues. While Canada's oil sands offer a possible future energy source for the EU, the negative environmental consequences of developing this resource are taken seriously by Europe, even as the current Canadian government focuses on their monetary potential.

The focus on economics is clear in a 2009 interview with Prime Minister Stephen Harper published in the French-language daily, *La Presse* on 8 May 2009. In the interview, Harper stated his vision of Canada as a "gateway to the North American market" for the EU. With repercussions from the financial crisis of 2008-2009 still being felt, such a vision could both decrease Canadian reliance on the USA and help increase the Canadian economy. Implicit in Harper's statement is the idea or hope that situating Canada in this manner would raise its strategic importance and relevance in the eyes of the two largest economic powers in the world. Harper's statement can also be seen as a wish to position Canada in relation to the EU's Lisbon treaty of 2009, which will enhance the EU's role in world political and economic affairs.

Conclusion

Canada and Europe are linked through a history of immigration and common heritage. The creation of a single European market has had obvious impact on Canadian trade relations; recent Canada-EU summits could have further major impact. Even if Stephen Harper's vision of Canada as a transit point between Europe and the USA does not become reality, Canada-EU relations will remain important. Europe is too large a market, and Canada too rich in natural resources, for the two parties to ignore each other. The question is whether Canada and Europe will be able to negotiate a free trade deal, and if so, will it actually come into effect or will it fall by the wayside, as was the case with Trudeau's framework agreement? Whatever the future trade relations between Canada and the EU, hopefully they will be mutually beneficial to the citizens of both.

References

AFP. 2009. Google News 12 May 2009. Retrieved 5 March 2010 from http://www.google.com/hostednews/afp/article/ALeqM5iFTBvThNTUxC1R9IvL8NicndDXKg

Beck, John. 1996. "Canada and the European Union." In Jim Hanson, & Susan McNish (eds.), *Canada's Strategic Interests in the New Europe*. Toronto: The Canadian Institute of Strategic Studies: (75 - 81).

Bothwell, Robert. 2007. *Alliance and Illusion: Canada and the World, 1945-1984*. Vancouver: UBC Press.

Christensen, R. B. (ed.). 1994. *Canada and the European Union - A Relationship in Focus*. Canada and the European Union - A Relationship in Focus, Toronto: The University of Toronto.

Granatstein, J. L., & Bothwell, Robert. 1990. *Pirouette: Pierre Trudeau and Canadian Foreign Policy*. Toronto: University of Toronto Press.

Hanson, Jim, & Susan McNish (eds.). 1996. *Canada's Strategic Interests in the New Europe*. Toronto: The Canadian Institute of Strategic Studies.

MacMillan, Gretchen M. (ed.). 1994. *The European Community, Canada and 1992*. Calgary: The University of Calgary.

Potter, Evan H. 1999. *Transatlantic Partners: Canadian Approaches to the European Union*. Montreal: McGill-Queen's University Press.

Sharp, Mitchell. 1972. "Canada-US Relations: Options for the Future," in: *International Perspectives* (28), 1-24.

Canada and the Netherlands in Afghanistan: a 3D Roadmap to Peace

Djeyhoun Ostowar

There has long been general consensus in Canada and the Netherlands about the main issues in Afghanistan. First, it is impossible to ignore major security threats coming from terrorist networks operating from Pakistan and Afghanistan. Second, the Afghan people deserve help after having suffered at the hands of the Taliban. Third, Afghanistan has to become a viable state where internal peace is maintained and where terrorists can never again find safe haven. Although the Dutch cabinet fell in February 2010 due to disagreements on extending the military deployment in Uruzgan province, these basic issues remain central.

Both the Dutch and Canadian contributions to the international mission in Afghanistan began with their participation in the US-led Operation Enduring Freedom after 9/11. Their roles later grew into a combined effort to fight against the Taliban insurgency and to pursue reconstruction efforts on the ground. Although the military struggle never ceased to be one of the main priorities, a great deal of resources, knowledge, and energy has gone into supporting Afghan government institutions and promoting the economic development of the country.

Since the move from a one-dimensional military mission to a wider agenda, both Canada and the Netherlands have adopted a so-called 3D approach of Defence, Development, and Diplomacy. This involves using the military only when absolutely necessary, creating safe areas for reconstruction efforts, investing in confidence building among the local population by providing for basic needs, and respecting their religious beliefs and traditions. This three-pillar approach is widely regarded as the most effective and sustainable way of addressing complex (post-) conflict situations such as those in Afghanistan. This essay addresses the merits of this strategy, particularly from the perspective of the Dutch and Canadian involvement in Afghanistan.

Military Intervention in Afghanistan

Afghanistan has endured more than three decades of armed conflict and widespread destruction since the violent coup in 1978, the Soviet military invasion of 1979, the civil war in the 1990s, and the short but extremely cruel Taliban regime. The Afghans have suffered enormously, and millions of

Djeyhoun Ostowar

people have been directly affected by the continuing violence. One of the most critical aspects of the conflict in Afghanistan is the enormous scale of human rights violations perpetrated by the opposing factions, not only against each other but, most importantly, against the civilian population as a whole.

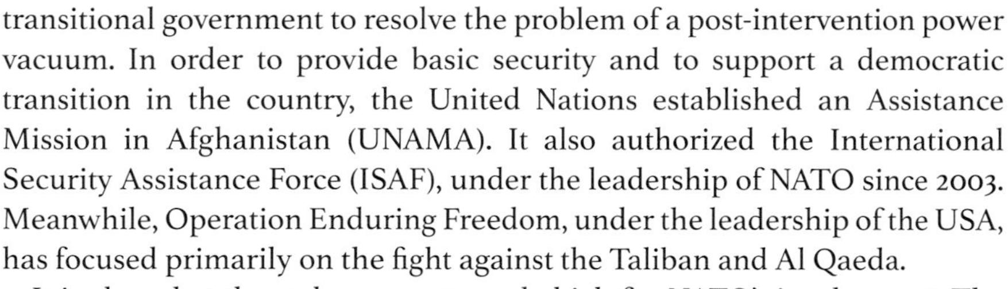

A major turning point came after the tragic events of 9/11, when more than 3000 people died in terrorist strikes by Al Qaeda operatives in New York City and Washington D.C.. Under US leadership, the allied forces launched a large-scale military intervention in Afghanistan, and the Taliban regime was quickly defeated. In late 2001, the Bonn Conference established a transitional government to resolve the problem of a post-intervention power vacuum. In order to provide basic security and to support a democratic transition in the country, the United Nations established an Assistance Mission in Afghanistan (UNAMA). It also authorized the International Security Assistance Force (ISAF), under the leadership of NATO since 2003. Meanwhile, Operation Enduring Freedom, under the leadership of the USA, has focused primarily on the fight against the Taliban and Al Qaeda.

It is clear that the stakes are extremely high for NATO's involvement. The alliance has made it one of its top priorities to bring peace and security to Afghanistan. As James Jones, the former NATO Supreme Allied Commander, commented: "In committing the alliance to sustained ground combat operations in Afghanistan NATO has bet its future. If NATO were to fail, alliance cohesion will be at grave risk. A moribund or unravelled NATO would have a profoundly negative geo-strategic impact" (Jones & Ullman, 2007).

Currently, more than 40 countries are contributing military and civilian personnel to the international mission in Afghanistan. Canada and the Netherlands are among the largest troop contributors, together with the United Kingdom, Germany, France, Italy, and, of course, the USA. The rationale for joining the mission has varied by country. For the Netherlands and Canada, it was a combination of the following considerations: meeting their multinational obligations under the UN, protecting their own national security, providing humanitarian assistance to the Afghan population, and development assistance for rebuilding a failed state.

To achieve some level of development beyond Kabul, it was decided to deploy Provincial Reconstruction Teams consisting of ISAF forces and civilian personnel. These work alongside the local and provincial authorities and international aid organizations. Effectiveness, efficiency, and good coordination of efforts are crucial aspects of the operation. There are many challenges that have to be addressed simultaneously. For this reason, the Afghan government and its international allies requested that certain countries lead in particular policy fields. The Canadians took on landmine clearance, the Dutch concentrated on supporting state institutions, the USA focused on training the Afghan National Army, and Germany initially took responsibility for training the police.

The 3D Approach in Afghanistan

The 3D approach is also known as whole-of-government approach. This comprehensive strategy for the reconstruction and sustainable development of war-torn societies is regarded as the most effective model for post-conflict peace-building missions. Neither a Canadian nor a Dutch invention, it has been used in various forms throughout history. The focus by Canada and the Netherlands on this approach in Afghanistan, however, has had a major impact on NATO thinking as a whole.

The 3D approach rests on the fundamental understanding that fragile states are a breeding ground for civil conflicts, terrorism, and regional instability – all of which can have terrible consequences for international peace and security. 9/11 was a clear illustration of what happens when the international community does not address the issue of weak states. In 2004, newly elected Canadian Prime Minister Paul Martin stated the following: "The three Ds mean building public institutions that work and are accountable to the public for their actions, 'not just policing' but also government ministries, a system of laws, courts, Human Rights Commissions, schools, hospitals, energy and water and transportation systems" (Martin, 2004). The success rate of reconstruction efforts, especially in a country like Afghanistan, is directly connected to how effectively the international community deals with the counter insurgency mission. The fight against militant combatants and for civilian development are inseparable parts of a larger post-conflict strategy.

Special aspects of the Dutch 3D approach include the so-called six-angle consultations and the civilian-military dual-command. All major decisions regarding the country's involvement in Afghanistan are made together by the Prime Minister, two Vice-Prime Ministers, the Minister of Foreign Affairs, the Minister of Defence, and the Minister of Development Cooperation. On a day-to-day basis there is interdepartmental integration with a dual-command in Uruzgan. All significant operational decisions are taken jointly by the military and civilian leaders. This strategy ensures that there are no separate or conflicting policies operating in Afghanistan.

The Dutch and Canadian policies regarding the reconstruction efforts in Uruzgan and Kandahar follow two parallel routes. At the macro level, the countries channel most of their aid funds to support and implement national and local programs in order to achieve greater legitimacy in the eyes of the Afghan population for the government in Kabul. At the micro level, by working closely together with NGOs and tribal leaders within the provinces, Canada and the Netherlands directly finance local projects concerning health care, education, and infrastructure.

Dutch forces in Operation Spin Ghar, Afghansitan, November 2007. Engineers leave for a patrol with the 13th Infantry Battalion Prince Bernhard.

The Strategy on the Ground

Afghanistan is certainly the largest Canadian international military operation since World War II. Most Canadian forces in Afghanistan, varying between 2200 and 2500 soldiers, are located in Kandahar. Since 2006, Canada has been in charge of the Provincial Reconstruction Team (PRT) Kandahar, which consists of civilian experts and several hundred soldiers. The deployed civilian personnel include diplomats representing the Canadian Ministry of Foreign Affairs, experts from the Canadian International Development Agency, and other specialists such as doctors and police officers.

In terms of scale and commitment, the situation is similar for the Netherlands. Between 1500 and 1800 soldiers are deployed, supported by six Apache helicopters, five Cougar transport helicopters, one C-130 transport airplane, and five F16 combat jets. Dutch troops are primarily situated in the province of Uruzgan. The military and the Provincial Reconstruction Team Uruzgan are supported by experienced civilian staff from the Department of Development Cooperation and the private sector. Like Canada, the Netherlands is challenged by operating in some of the poorest, underdeveloped, and unstable areas of the country.

The Afghan government needs to increase its control in these provinces, but it can only do so if it is able to provide basic security and services for the people. ISAF has to ensure that there is some level of stability before aid organisations can start their activities and before actual reconstruction can commence. To achieve this objective, the ISAF adopted the "ink-spot" strategy. Once control is established in carefully chosen locations, it is gradually extended to neighbouring districts. On the operational level, the main challenge is to sustain control over a longer period of time, at the same time increasing popular support for the international forces and the Afghan government. For the PRT Uruzgan, for instance, the ISAF first launched an offensive against insurgents in the strategically important town of Tarin Kowt, where it then established a permanent base. With a strong ISAF presence, this area has been kept relatively safe, and the PRT gradually expanded to new towns and districts. Locations to be included in the "ink spot" undergo close investigation by military intelligence, their civilian colleagues, and the Afghan authorities. The aim is to find out more about the population's most pressing needs and the level of their support for the insurgency. Only after a thorough investigation does ISAF command begin its military operations against insurgents. Once the area is confirmed as safe, the Afghan authorities and reconstruction teams can start their activities. But the threat from insurgency often disappears only temporarily. The Taliban and insurgents regularly use intimidation and terror to scare the local population. Despite this problem, the PRTs establish conditions for dialogue with local leaders, providing safe storage for impounded weapons and the implementation of development projects. This way, the local people can see that ISAF soldiers and the Afghan authorities are interested in helping them.

Building trust, in the sense of "winning hearts and minds," has been central to Dutch and Canadian operations from the outset. Soldiers build up communication with the local population and actively help with repairing bridges and school buildings, increasing medical supplies, and restoring access to clean water. PRT command maintains direct contact with local tribal and religious leaders. Mutual trust not only helps reconstruction efforts to succeed, but also increases the safety of the soldiers themselves. If there are good relations between the military and the population, the Afghans are less likely to support the insurgents or be intimidated by them. Obviously, the operation's success in this struggle is undermined when reconstruction projects are seriously delayed, or more importantly, when military operations lead to accidental civilian deaths or injury. NATO's air strike in Uruzgan in February 2010 is a recent example: mistakenly, the USA targeted a non-military convoy of vehicles and killed 27 civilians. This caused widespread resentment and protest in Kabul and in the province itself (www.bbc.co.uk). Hence, from the strategic point of view, too, it is vital to minimize threats to the civilian population.

Since relatively recently, more emphasis has been placed on Afghan ownership and the transfer of responsibility. This primarily means the Afghanization of military operations. There is now close cooperation between ISAF, the Afghan National Army, and the police. The increasing visibility of Afghan forces contributes not only to security but also helps legitimize the Afghan national government. Improving the capacity of the Afghan security sector is vital because international forces are already overstretched, and they will not remain for an indefinite period of time. The fall of the Dutch cabinet in February 2010 almost certainly means that the Dutch military will leave Uruzgan by the end of the year. Meanwhile, the Canadian mission ends in July 2011 and soldiers are likely to be withdrawn by the end of that year.

Investing in the Future of Afghanistan

The Afghanistan Compact, which was the outcome of the London Conference on Afghanistan in 2006, drew up a five-year international strategy for the country. In line with this international political commitment, Canada has set ambitious objectives for reducing female unemployment by 20% and clearing around 70% (approximately 500 square kilometres) of Afghanistan's mine-contaminated land (www.cbc.ca). As part of the demilitarization process, Canada has helped the Afghan government and the United Nations to find and safely store thousands of weapons including heavy artillery and rocket launchers. There is currently an operational National Army headquarters in Kandahar and hundreds of Afghan soldiers and policemen have already completed their training. There are more than 20 checkpoints and sub-stations to carry out daily security operations.

The non-military aspect, however, also forms a significant part of Canadian activity in Kandahar. Canada's total spending on Afghanistan (2001-2011) amounts to $ 1.9 billion, making Afghanistan the single largest recipient of Canadian bilateral support. Part of the Canadian aid money was invested in micro-loans for the Afghans. Already more than 580 micro-loans have been distributed, with almost 90% of the recipients being women. Each year, Afghanistan receives several million dollars in humanitarian aid from Canada. Some 350,000 children in Kandahar have been vaccinated against polio. Twelve schools have been built and another 21 are under construction. More than 550,000 people are recipients of food aid through the World Food Program, partly financed by Canada (www.afghanistan.gc.ca). Furthermore, Canada supports the large Dahla Dam and irrigation project, which is expected to improve the agricultural sector and provide temporary jobs.

The Netherlands has also been a generous donor to the mission in Afghanistan. Since 2006, the Netherlands has invested approximately 300 million euros in Afghan development. More than one-third of the financing is committed to Uruzgan alone (www.netherlands-embassy.org). The Netherlands is one of the leading contributors to the World Bank Reconstruction Trust Fund, created primarily to cover the costs of rebuilding the Afghan government, including salaries, technical facilities, and other administrative activities. The Netherlands is also among the main contributors to the Law and Order Trust Fund for Afghanistan, which finances the maintenance of the Afghan police force

Currently there are more than 180 medical care stations in Uruzgan and almost everyone has access to basic health care. Around 43,000 children, of whom approximately 4,000 are girls, attend school (www.minbuza.nl). Millions of Euros are invested in improving the agricultural sector as it is the most important pillar of the Afghan economy. Through sharing agricultural expertise, irrigation projects, and rebuilding basic infrastructure, the Netherlands aims to improve the livelihood of the local population. Examples of successfully implemented 3D operations include Mani Ghar, Tura Ghar, and Deh Rawood. Certainly the most remarkable case, though, is the district of Chora. In 2007, it was under the control of insurgents and lacked any governance structures. Now it is one of the most stable districts in south Afghanistan.

Conclusion

Afghanistan remains one of the most troubled and least developed countries in the world. The rates of infant and maternal mortality, unemployment, illiteracy, and corruption are extremely high. In recent years, fighting has intensified, the number of civilian and military casualties has increased, and the drug trade remains untamed. Afghanistan faces major problems with the effectiveness of governance, the rule of law, and reconciliation processes. Nonetheless, in almost nine years of joint effort, visible progress has been achieved both at the national level and in the provinces. Even though there is no flourishing democracy in Afghanistan, it is possible to speak of concrete positive results in the field of security, governance, and development.

Since 2001, Afghanistan has managed to establish reasonably well-functioning governmental institutions. The Provincial Councils and the Wolesi Jirga (legislative National Assembly) are directly elected bodies that shape legislation and exercise political control over the ministries. An independent judicial branch is in place to protect the constitution and the rule of law in general. There is, however, a lack of trained legal professionals and enforcement agencies. The elections of 2004-2005 can be considered a major step forward in the democratization of Afghanistan. Approximately six-and-a-half million Afghans voted, without major outbreaks of violence. The candidates came from different ethnic groups and levels of society. Dozens of women were elected to the national parliament and provincial councils (Kippen, 2008). Unfortunately, the elections in Afghanistan still face serious setbacks due to widespread corruption and weak vetting procedures. A much more consistent implementation of vetting laws and closer monitoring by the UN and other partners could help make the Parliamentary Elections of 2010 more successful.

Much has been invested and achieved in the security sector. In 2001, Afghanistan had virtually no army or functioning police; instead there were separate militias and privately-run armed groups. With the help of the international community, and in particular of the USA, NATO and the EU, Afghanistan has organized around 95,000 soldiers and more than 80,000 police officers. The aim is to increase their numbers even further and to provide them with necessary training and equipment. Within the next five years, Afghan security forces must be capable of relieving the burden of the country's security, thereby reducing and eventually completely eliminating the need for international forces to be present in Afghanistan.

NATO's emphasis on the 3D approach illustrates that military and police action alone is not enough to bring peace and progress to Afghanistan. Major international conferences in Paris in June 2008, in The Hague in March 2009, and in London in January 2010 have all reconfirmed the commitment of the international community to Afghanistan's development. By now, thousands of kilometres of roads have been built, forming important linkages for regional and international trade. Hundreds of new schools and clinics have been constructed, as well as dozens of power plants, bridges, and dams. There are international trade and investment agreements directed towards increasing Afghan economic growth. The telecommunication sector is flourishing with dozens of new and independent television and radio channels, newspapers, and magazines. Each year more and more Afghans have access to internet and telephones.

It is true that Afghanistan still has a long way to go, but at least people have reason to be optimistic. There is renewed hope for a better future. To realize their objectives, however, Afghans need to count on a long-lasting commitment by their international partners. In this context, the Netherlands' and Canada's future investments in the development and reconstruction of Afghanistan are crucial.

References

Afghanistan Research and Evaluation Unit. 2008. Elections in 2009 and 2010: Technical and Contextual Challenges to Building Democracy In Afghanistan. [Briefing Paper Series]. Kabul: Grant Kippen.

BBC. 2010. "Afghanistan condemns deadly Nato air strike in Uruzgan." Retrieved from http://news.bbc.co.uk/2/hi/8528715.stm

CBC News. 2009. "Canada in Afghanistan." Retrieved 10 February 2009 from http://www.cbc.ca/canada/story/2009/02/10/f-afghanistan.html

Gabriëlse, Robbert. 2009. A 3D Approach to Security and Development

http://www.regjeringen.no/upload/UD/Vedlegg/FN/Multidimensional%20and%20Integrated/A%203D%20Approach%20to%20Security%20and%20Development.pdf

Government of Canada: Canada's Approach in Afghanistan http://www.afghanistan.gc.ca/canada-afghanistan/approach-approche/index.aspx?menu_id=1&menu=L

Jones, James and Harlan Ullman. 2007. "What Is at Stake in Afghanistan," letter to *TheWashington Post*, 10 April 2007.

Martin, Paul. 2004. "Address by Prime Minister Paul Martin on Occasion of His Visit to Washington D.C," Washington, D.C, 29 April 2004.

Netherlands Ministry of Foreign Affairs. 2010. Afghanistan. Retrieved 21 February 2010 from http://www.minbuza.nl/nl/Onderwerpen/Afghanistan

The Netherlands in Afghanistan: A 3D Approach Defense, Development and Diplomacy http://www.netherlands-embassy.org/files/pdf/AfghanistanFactsheetDecember09.pdf

The ICC's First Decade:

the Role of the Netherlands and Canada in the First Permanent International Criminal Court

Arlinda Rrustemi

Arlinda Rrustemi

After 16 years in the international legal capital, The Hague, the International Criminal Tribunal for the Former Yugoslavia (ICTY) will finish its work by 2012. Similar to its *ad hoc* counterparts, namely the Special Court for Sierra Leone (SCSL) and the International Criminal Tribunal for Rwanda, the ICTY has been regarded as mostly successful. Although only temporary in nature, these courts have created a long-lasting legacy in the awareness that the gravest human rights abuses need to be brought to justice. The wars in the Balkan region and in Africa during the 1990s underlined the necessity for a more established legal body that could deal with genocide, war crimes, and crimes against humanity on a permanent basis. This idea was not new. Following World War II and the Holocaust, the UN General Assembly adopted a resolution establishing an International Law Commission to draw up a statute for an international criminal court. Article VI of the Genocide Convention was to be the basis for this work. Cold War politics put these ambitious plans on ice.

More than four decades later, the plans for an international court were revived. In 1998, after many formal and informal negotiations, 120 states adopted the Rome Statute, establishing the first permanent International Criminal Court (ICC) in history (Schabas, 2007: ix). As described by the Court's former president, the Canadian Philippe Kirsch, on the tenth anniversary of the adoption of the Rome Statute, this was "the culmination of fifty years of efforts to establish a permanent criminal court" as well as "a remarkable achievement on the part of international diplomacy" (ICC, 2009). As this essay will show, both the Netherlands and Canada played central roles in designing and implementing the Court.

Jurisdiction and Structure of the ICC

As with any other judicial body, the first important questions to ask are "what kind of cases are dealt with?" and "who can address the Court?" Article 5 of the Rome Statute of the ICC permits the prosecution of criminals on four grounds: genocide, war crimes, crimes against humanity, and the crime of aggression. The last basis is still not clearly defined. However, the other three grounds are defined and recognized, partly also on the basis of the case law provided by the *ad hoc* tribunals previously mentioned. The question of whether the ICC has jurisdiction in a specific case is also decided on the grounds of territory and nationality (Schabas, 2007: 58). The Court can only address crimes that have been committed by citizens of a State Party or that have taken place on its territory. The jurisdiction of the ICC can be instated by various means, respectively the Security Council, the *proprio motu* power of the Prosecutor (meaning that he can initiate a case out of his own motion), and referral of the Party States themselves. As of early 2010 there have been four cases, related to situations in northern Uganda, the Democratic Republic of the Congo, the Central African Republic, and Darfur. Whereas the first three situations were triggered by state referral, the last one was based on a UN Security Council decision which called for an investigation into the situation in Sudan.

Membership in the ICC is open to any state that is willing to adhere to the Rome Statute. Thus far, 110 states have ratified the Statute, a sufficient mandate to activate the Court's jurisdiction. The Court operates as an independent body with its own working apparatus: a Presidency, Judicial Divisions/Chambers, Office of the Prosecutor, Registry, Coordination Council and Advisory Committees. The ICC differs from previous *ad hoc* tribunals in that it controls funds for compensation and other services for victims, such as the Trust Fund for Victims, the Victims and Witnesses Unit, and the Office of Public Counsel for Victims. This careful treatment of the victims themselves is viewed as one of the positive features of the ICC, comparable to the provisions that victims receive in domestic criminal courts.

Host and Supporter: the Role of the Netherlands

The first essential contribution of the Netherlands to the ICC was the offer of a location. The trials and appeals of the ICC take place in The Hague, the legal capital of the world, according to Krieken and McCay (2005). The Court is part of a long tradition of international courts and bodies that operate and have operated in The Hague, creating a distinct international judicial atmosphere in this city. Other institutions operating in The Hague include the International Court of Justice, the ICTY, and the Permanent Court of Arbitration. Article 3(1) of the Rome Statute names the Netherlands as the "home of the court", although Article 3(3) provides that the seat of the Court may change if this is desirable. There is no indication, however, why such a development should take place. The construction of the ICC's permanent premises has not yet begun. It is currently seated in a temporary building in the east of The Hague.

As the "international community" occupies no specified territory, there have been discussions concerning where sentences given by the Court should be served. The State Parties to the Rome Statute share the responsibility in

Courtesy Michel Veenman

The Hague International Criminal Court building established at the beginning of 21th century as the first permanent court over four crimes, crimes against humanity, war crimes, crimes of aggression, and genocide.

Courtesy Anke Teunissen

Vredespaleis [Peace Palace] in the legal capital of the world, The Hague.

this respect, and the Netherlands volunteered to provide its services. The UN Detention Unit, or Temporary Detention Unit, offered by the Netherlands, is located in the Haaglanden Prison near Scheveningen, a district of The Hague. The ICC currently has twelve cells at its disposal. This practical assistance is provident; two indicted war criminals are currently incarcerated there: Thomas Lubanga and Charles Taylor (the latter being prosecuted at the SCSL). The Unit may be inspected by independent bodies, such as the International Committee of the Red Cross, at any time. The logistical support offered by the Netherlands has functioned well during the first ten years of the ICC.

Dutch involvement, though, goes further than simply offering a location and facilities. During discussions about the establishment of "a unique investigative opportunity" (meaning that documents need to be assessed independently within a period of six months), the Prosecutor suggested that the Netherlands Forensic Institute (NFI) should be included in the process, as it was known to act independently, impartially, and objectively, with very high academic standards. The NFI is an independent expert body within the Dutch Ministry of Justice (Schabas, 2007: 254). Despite the fact that the Institute had no connection to the Court or the Prosecutor, it quickly showed its readiness to perform this task. The Pre-Trial Chamber also supported the Prosecutor's suggestion, stating that the NFI could scientifically assess such documents. Since then, there has been close collaboration between the Institute and the Prosecutor. The general willingness of various institutions within the Netherlands to support the Court has reaffirmed the decision to locate the ICC in The Hague.

While the Dutch government was involved throughout the whole process of establishing the Court, special mention should be given to the Preparatory Committees (PrepCom) established by the UN General Assembly on 11 December 1995. The enormous task of the PrepCom was to draft a statute for states to consider at the general conference on the creation of the Court. Essential notions of the ICC, such as the principle of complementarity between national courts and the ICC, were set out during this phase. The work of the PrepCom lasted for almost three years, from 1995 to 1998, and was chaired throughout the process by Adriaan Bos, then senior Legal Adviser of the Dutch Ministry of Foreign Affairs. The contribution made by the Dutch delegation was immense. A year after the successful conference, a book was published with contributions from renowned international justices, such as Rosalyn Higgins and Canadian Louise Arbour, emphasizing Bos's contribution. Philippe Kirsch, the Court's first President, summarized it as follows: "The preparatory negotiations would not have progressed as far as they did without the leadership of Adriaan Bos. His determination, his thorough understanding of the subject, and his personal commitment, along with the efforts of the entire Dutch delegation, kept the momentum behind a project which once was thought impossible" (von Hebel, Lammers, and Schuking, 1999: 2).

Leading the "like-minded": the Contribution of Canada

Canada's contribution has been very visible since the establishment of the ICC. From the beginning, Canada was a leader of those states determined to secure funding and bring the Court into existence. It also contributed in more specific matters, from bringing an end to jurisdictional impunity (those responsible for major human rights abuses must be held accountable for their deeds), to initiating accountability campaigns, and to the practical implementation of the legal body. Canada committed considerable resources and advocacy to the plan to realize the ICC. As in the case of the Dutch, the most illustrative example of Canadian input is the contribution of one individual, Philippe Kirsch, who has been a leading figure throughout the early history of the Court. During the Rome Conference, Kirsch was the chair of the Committee of the Whole, the primary negotiating body. Later, he became one of the first judges to the Court and the ICC's first President from 2003 until 2009.

The so-called "like-minded group" (LMG), a coalition of around 60 "middle powers and developing countries, a number of which had directly suffered from some of the crimes described" (Kirsch and Holmes, 1999: 4), had been active since the first session of the PrepCom. Both the Netherlands and Canada were part of the LMG, with Canada chairing the influential coalition for nearly a decade. Canada gave up the chair only when Philippe Kirsch became President of the Conference Committee as a whole (Schabas, 2007: 19). The main aim of the LMG, and of Canada in particular, was to convince others to join in the process of creating a Court. The LMG held the view that the Court should be given jurisdiction over the gravest imaginable crimes, a category that, according to the LMG, includes the four crimes that are mentioned in the Statute today. They called for the elimination of the veto powers of the permanent members of the Security Council on prosecutions in order to decrease political influence in the workings of the Court. Finally, the LMG states planned to foster the independence of the Court by giving the Prosecutor the power to initiate proceedings *propriu motu* – an idea that was highly contested during the negotiations. In the end, it was a strong, independent, and viable Court that LMG countries envisaged.

Evidently, many of the issues proposed by the "like-minded group" were successfully taken up in the Rome Statute. The three types of crimes prosecuted nowadays are those proposed by the LMG coalition, and the crime of aggression will be assessed further in an upcoming conference later this year [2010]. While the coalition also secured an independent prosecutor with powers to initiate proceedings out of his own motion, Article 16 of the Statute gives the UN Security Council the power to defer the investigations of the prosecutor for a period of 12 months (with the possibility for further deferral thereafter). Twelve years since the successful adoption of the Rome Statute, the LMG coalition is still active, now as an informal group of diplomats that is called "Friends of the Court" (Schabas, 2007: 367). The group meets irregularly, mostly when the Court is confronted with problems that ought to be addressed on the political level. It also promotes the cooperation of states with investigations and the general awareness of the ICC and its activities.

As a member and leader of the LMG, Canada has supported an independent and effective ICC through lobbying and organizing public advocacy events. Canada also contributed to the UN Trust Fund, which enabled developing countries to participate in the ICC negotiations (Canada, 2009). In this way, it was ensured that a majority of the states of the world was represented at the negotiation table. It also fostered the participation of NGOs, who provided essential expertise during the Rome Conference (see CICC, 2005). Later, many victims from developing countries benefited from the Fund. The extent of Canadian support indicates a serious intent "not simply to establish the court, but to ensure that it is one worth having" (UN, 2008).

At times, Canada has advanced its own views, even if these were not completely in line with the standpoint of the LMG. For example, during the Rome Conference there was much discussion on the provisions of Article 12 concerning jurisdiction. The final provision sets out four crimes, as well as issues of territory and nationality of the person committing the crimes in question. There were disagreements on this Article between those states that are experiencing conflict situations, and those that are not. Most of the states involved in wars at the time rejected the idea of territorial jurisdiction, whereas Canada, the Scandinavian countries, Ireland, and the Netherlands lobbied strongly for it. Despite powerful adversaries such as the USA, the final outcome was a victory for those advocating a progressive notion of territorial jurisdiction, as this was included in Article 12(a) of the Statute. Ensuring that the ICC could also prosecute nationals of a non-State Party on the grounds of territory made the Court eventually "a promising and realistic mechanism capable of addressing civil conflict, human rights abuses and war" (Schabas, 2007: 62). Against all odds, many states ratified the ICC Statute precisely for this reason, making the efforts of Canada and the Netherlands doubly important. In the end, the ICC was truly a Court "worth having."

Conclusion

Today, more than ten years after its establishment, the International Criminal Court has become a powerful institution for the prosecution of justice. Hardly imaginable two decades ago, it is a permanent court that protects people in over 110 countries around the world, against war crimes and grave human rights abuses. In realizing this very ambitious project, the contributions of the Netherlands and Canada have been essential. The Netherlands is the host state of the Court, providing it a place in the recognized legal capital of the world. It provides essential services with the Netherlands Forensic Institute and the Detention Unit in Scheveningen. Dutch input into the PrepCom, in particular through senior Legal Advisor Adriaan Bos, was also vital.

The role of Canada has likewise been considerable. As one of the most influential states of the "like-minded group", its significance can be traced back to its leadership of the coalition, support for funding, and determination to ensure a permanent, independent, and meaningful legal body. The Canadian Judge Philippe Kirsch was a key figure during the negotiations and led the Court as President during its first phase. Although it is clear that the Court will face many challenges in the future, the commitment of Canada and the Netherlands has already established the ICC as a serious body able to meet the ambitious aims set out in the Rome Statute.

References

Coalition for the International Criminal Court. 2005. Commemorative Messages on the occasion of the tenth anniversary of the NGO Coalition for the International Criminal Court. Retrieved 13 March 2005 from http://www.coalitionfortheicc.org/documents/10thAnnCommemMessages10Feb05.pdf

Foreign Affairs and International Trade Canada. 2009. "Canada and the Court." Retrieved 13 March 2005 from http://www.international.gc.ca/court-cour/icc-canada-cpi.aspx?lang=eng&menu_id=62&menu=R

Hebel, Herman von, Johan G. Lammers, Jolien Schuking (eds.). 1999. *Reflections on the International Criminal Court: essays in honour of Adriaan Bos*. The Hague: T.M.C. Asser Press.

International Criminal Court. 2009. Tenth anniversary of the adoption of the Rome Statute of the International Criminal Court. Retrieved 7 March 2009 from http://www.icc-cpi.int/iccdocs/asp_docs/ASP7/10th/ICC-ASP-10thAnni-Kirsch-ENG.pdf

Kirsch, Philippe, and John T. Holmes. 1999. "The Rome Conference on an International Criminal Court: The Negotiating Process." *The American Journal of International Law* 93, no. 1: 2-12.

Kirsch, Philippe. 1999. "Introduction." In Herman von Hebel, Johan G. Lammers, Jolien Schuking (eds.). *Reflections on the International Criminal Court: essays in honour of Adriaan Bos*. The Hague: T.M.C. Asser Press.

Krieken, Peter J. and David McKay. 2005. *The Hague - Legal Capital of the World*. Cambridge: Cambridge University Press.

Schabas, William. 2007. *An Introduction to the International Criminal Court*. Cambridge: Cambridge University Press.

United Nations. 1998. Diplomatic Conference: four days of general statements on establishment of international criminal court. Retrieved 10 March 1998 from http://www.un.org/icc/pressrel/lrom7.htm

Introduction

The Road to Radboud – Nijmegen and Canada

Hans Bak
Radboud University, Nijmegen

In December 1944, Canadian poet Earle Birney travelled the war-mangled "Road to Nijmegen" in an army jeep, searching in vain for transcendence (except perhaps in the "rainbow answer" of a woman's eyes) amidst a war-wrecked Dutch landscape: "bones of tanks beside the stoven bridges," "women riding into the wind on the rims of their cycles," "clusters of children, like flies ... groping in gravel for knobs of coal/ their legs standing like dead stems out of their clogs" ("The Road to Nijmegen," 1946). Today, a large Canadian War Cemetery near Nijmegen, close to the National Liberation Museum at Groesbeek, bears witness to the impressive contribution made by Canadian soldiers to the liberation of the region during and after Operation Market Garden – a human sacrifice still firmly embedded in Nijmegen's cultural memory. Since then, numerous Canadian soldiers and civilians annually walk "The Road to Nijmegen" in a more peaceful light, as participants in the Four Day Marches, cheered on by a local population whose images of Canadian veterans and war brides come from national commemorations or popular Dutch television series such as "The Summer of '45" rather than from personal memory or wartime stories.

For the younger Dutch generation, born 35 years or more after the war, Canada readily evokes stereotypical images of lakes and pine trees, Mounties and moose, beavers and maple leaves, igloos and "Eskimos", ice hockey and snow – and, for animal rights' supporters, seals. Other images or associations with Canada are likely to come from global popular culture, be it movies or music – Michael J. Fox, Jim Carey, Celine Dion, Leonard Cohen, Neil Young, Alanis Morissette, Rufus Wainwright. For many decades, Canadian writers, intellectuals, and politicians have done much to subvert and complicate these stereotypes. As a result, Dutch students often feel affinity with Canada, perhaps especially with its critical and ambiguous relationship with its powerful southern neighbour, appreciating its role as "the dispassionate witness" (David Staines) and relishing the fact that some of America's sharpest critics have been Canadian. The Canada they have come to see is an active and influential player on the global scene – a nation on the cutting edge of developments in international politics, law, and economics, in communications and technology, in ecology and environmentalism, and in multiculturalism and migration. In many of these areas, they feel, Canada has played a pioneering role, ambitious to present itself as a possible "blueprint" for a new world order, speaking to a unifying Europe, and offering a viable alternative to the role historically, but also controversially, played by the USA.

There are, then, good reasons why interest in Canada should have found a foothold at Radboud University in Nijmegen. For many years, Dr. Cornelius Remie, founding father of Canadian Studies in the Netherlands, taught about Canada in his field of cultural anthropology, organizing a major polar expedition to northern Canada on the occasion of the university's 70th anniversary in 1993. A recipient of one of Canada's Meritorious Service medals in 1998, he was president of the Association for Canadian Studies in the Netherlands (ACSN) as well as of the International Council for Canadian Studies (ICCS) and a driving force in the European Network for Canadian Studies. From 1983, the teaching of Canadian history, first by Dr. Hardy Beekelaar, later by Dr. Jac Geurts, has been an integral part of the Nijmegen curriculum. My personal involvement with Canadian literature was a journey from ignorance to enthusiasm. It began with a phone call in 1993 from a Dutch publishing firm, *De Geus*, asking if I would be interested in a guest lecture by a Canadian author: Carol Shields. "Carol who?" was my embarrassing response.

Well-known in Canada, Carol Shields was in the Netherlands to promote the translation of her 1992 novel, *The Republic of Love*. Her visit to Nijmegen coincided with the very day of the announcement that she had won the Governor General's Award for Fiction, Canada's highest literary prize, for her 1993 novel, *The Stone Diaries*. This book launched me on an ongoing reading exploration of Canadian literature; it has been on the syllabus of Nijmegen students ever since.

Since 1993, with the help of ACSN and ICCS, a galaxy of Canadian writers and scholars has travelled "the Road to Nijmegen" to help give shape and substance to the teaching of Canadian Studies – Matt Cohen, Cyril Dabydeen, Elizabeth Hay, Aritha van Herk, Isabel Huggan, Wayne Johnston, Janice Kulyk Keefer, John Lennox, David Staines, Guy Vanderhaeghe, and Christl Verduyn, as well as the British Canadian literature specialist, Coral Ann Howells. Nijmegen hosted the 1998 ACSN symposium, "Canadian Unity: Facts and F(r)ictions", and provided the impetus behind a three-day international conference on "First Nations of North America: Politics and Representation" in 2002, the proceedings of which were published under the conference title by VU University Press in 2005.

Nijmegen students have conducted research for their Master's theses at the University of Guelph and Simon Fraser University, and in 2001 an exchange agreement was established with the University of Ottawa. Nijmegen staff has participated in ICCS seminars in Ottawa, Calgary, and Vancouver. As president of ACSN (2000-2003), I was privileged to attend meetings of the ICCS, which sponsored an internship in Canadian Studies at Nijmegen in 2002. Indeed, is it entirely coincidental that the present Dutch ambassador to Canada, Willem Geerts, is a Nijmegen graduate?

Unmistakably, a momentum was building. It peaked in 2005 with the launch of a Minor program in Canadian Studies: “Focus on Canada”. Supported by the Faculty of Arts and Letters, and co-financed by ICCS and DFAIT, the program featured courses in Canadian history and literature, as well as an interdisciplinary seminar in Canadian politics, business, and society. In May 2005, former Governor General Adrienne Clarkson, accompanied by John Ralston Saul and the Canadian ambassador to the Netherlands, Serge April, visited Nijmegen to officially inaugurate the Minor.

Since then, student interest in Canada at Radboud University, Nijmegen, has continued to be strong. At present, 67 students are taking courses in Canadian history and literature. The three contributors to this section have all been inspired by their studies of Canada at Radboud University to develop strong personal and professional links to Canada: Hans van Riet as an inveterate explorer of Canada’s north, Irene Salverda as a researcher into the political and legal struggles of First Nations peoples in British Columbia, and Ruben Vroegop as a prospective Canadian citizen and an analyst with the Department of National Defence in Ottawa. All three show themselves to be “passionate witnesses” in their essays, if always from an ineradicably Dutch perspective.

The World's Most Impressive Highway

Hans van Riet

On 4 February 2000, I took a flight from Amsterdam to Vancouver, British Columbia. After roughly ten hours, I arrived at Vancouver Airport, setting foot on Canadian soil for the first time. That two-week trip was to be the first of many I would take to and through Canada in the years since. I have visited Canada at least once a year since 2000, sometimes for as long as two months. My last visit was in February and March 2009, when I travelled from Vancouver to the province of Saskatchewan. In August 2010, I plan to explore the province of Manitoba. It will be my 12th expedition to Canada in ten years. Since my very first encounter with Canada and Canadians, I have been determined to explore as much of the vast country as possible, both physically and intellectually. The latter goal became possible when, in September 2005, I commenced the Canadian Studies Minor program, "Focus on Canada: Introduction to Canadian Studies", at Radboud University in Nijmegen.

This essay concerns the road that took me on a trip through the most magnificent landscape that I have ever seen, and on the most challenging journey that I have ever undertaken. In August 2005, accompanied by my girlfriend, I set out from Vancouver to the city of Inuvik in Canada's Northwest Territories. The final stretch of what I have come to think of as an epic journey was over the Dempster Highway. Below, I will discuss the location of this 671-kilometre (417-mile) road through the Arctic wilderness. Then, I will elaborate on the history of the person the highway is named after: Inspector William John Duncan Dempster of the Royal Canadian Mounted Police (RCMP). Following this, I will expand on the history of the building of the highway. And finally, I will briefly discuss my own experiences of this truly incredible road: a Dutch explorer's impression of the Canadian North.

The Geographical Location

Where does the "real north" begin and what is it like? Perhaps the answer lies along the Dempster Highway, as this is the only road in Canada that takes you across the Arctic Circle and into the true "Land of the Midnight Sun". The Dempster Highway is a 671-kilometre road through the Arctic wilderness, starting about 40 kilometres east of Dawson City in the Yukon and ending in Inuvik in the Northwest Territories. From Dawson City, the road heads north over the Ogilvie and Richardson Mountains, connecting the villages of Eagle

Hans van Riet

Plains, Fort McPherson, Tsiigehtchic, and Inuvik, and linking the Klondike Highway in the Yukon to the Mackenzie River delta in the Northwest Territories. The road, which makes motorized travel along the full length of North America possible, is also referred to as Northwest Territories Highway 8 or Yukon Highway 5.

During the winter months, the road extends another 194 kilometres to Tuktoyaktuk, Northwest Territories, on the northern coast of Canada. Under the name "Tuktoyaktuk Winter Road", it uses frozen portions of the Mackenzie River delta as an ice road; this extension of the road is not, however, considered to be a "real" part of the Dempster Highway. The highway crosses two major rivers: the Peel River and the Mackenzie River. One crosses these rivers by ferry in summertime and by ice bridge in wintertime. The Dempster Highway is thus Canada's only all-weather road to cross the Arctic Circle. It also crosses two minor rivers: the Ogilvie and Eagle rivers, by two bridges. Part of the road leads through the magnificent Tombstone Territorial Park, a wildlife reserve established in 1999, which protects 2,165 square kilometres. A substantial section of the road tracks an old dog-sled trail, roughly following the route of William John Duncan Dempster, who gave his name to the highway. Moreover, the road leads into an exceptional landscape dominated by permafrost and its flora and fauna. Permafrost is soil that has been at or below the freezing point of water for two or more years. Often, though not always, there is ice in quantities which may exceed the earth's potential for hydraulic saturation. Permafrost exists in 24% of exposed land in the northern hemisphere. Plant life can be supported only within the active surface layer, since growth can occur only in soil that is fully thawed for at least part of the year. The formation of permafrost thus has major effects on ecological systems, first and foremost on plants but also on fauna requiring subsurface homes, such as rabbits and moles. Black Spruce is dominant, since this species of tree can root in thin surface soil. With wide open valleys contrasted by sharp mountain ranges, and rivers cutting through the vast open tundra, the scenery is amazing.

The Dempster Highway runs through the lands of several First Nations peoples, including the Han, Gwitchin, and Inuvialuit. Approximately 20,000 years ago, the ancestors of these peoples came over the Bering Strait, a land bridge at that time, through Alaska to the Yukon and Northwest Territories. Thus, the territory on which the Dempster Highway is located is also the oldest populated area of Canada, which makes it even more exciting to cross.

What's in a Name?

The Dempster Highway is named after Inspector William John Duncan Dempster of the Royal Canadian Mounted Police (RCMP). Dempster was born in Wales on 21 October 1876. He immigrated to Canada in 1897 and joined

Courtesy Babette van den Berg.

Arctic Tundra Environment.

the North-West Mounted Police. The Canadian Government established the North-West Mounted Police in 1873 to act as its quasi-military agent in the west. In 1898, during the Klondike Gold Rush, the RCMP posted Dempster in the Yukon, where he would remain for the rest of his career. In 1934, he retired at the rank of Inspector and moved to Vancouver, where he died in 1964.

In his early career years as a Corporal, Dempster frequently ran the dog sled trail from Dawson City to Fort McPherson. In wintertime, he patrolled this route personally. He completed the 765-kilometre expedition ten times in four years. The route was considered very difficult but safe to traverse. It followed a complicated series of rivers and creeks and flat, treeless valleys, as well as stretches of rocky terrain. Today's highway follows roughly the same original trail. Because Dempster undertook the journey under even the roughest and toughest of circumstances, such as temperatures of 40 degrees below zero, he became known as "The Iron Man of the Trail". Dempster himself learned the trail from the Gwitchin First Nations peoples, who lived (and still live) in the region. It was their main transportation link between the Yukon and the Peel river systems, serving to transport goods to trade first with other First Nations tribes and later with white traders. The trail was subsequently used by the North-West Mounted Police to carry mail and news, and to carry out the law.

Dempster became a prominent Canadian historical figure in the winter of 1911. In February of that year, he was chosen to lead the search for the famous

Courtesy Babette van den Berg.

View of the Dempster Highway.

"Lost Patrol" of Inspector F.J. Fitzgerald. Travelling southwest from Fort McPherson in 1910-1911, without a First Nations guide, Fitzgerald followed the trail in reverse, but lost his way near the headwaters of Little Wind River. When the Inspector did not arrive at the expected time in Dawson City, Dempster was ordered to find and rescue the patrol. He headed to the village of Fort McPherson and soon discovered signs that the patrol had lost its way. At old campsites, he noticed obvious signs of trouble, such as an abandoned dog harness and "the paws of a dog cut off at the knee joint, also a shoulder blade which had been cooked and the flesh evidently eaten." On 21 and 22 March, Dempster discovered that all the members of the patrol had died trying to return to Fort McPherson. As a result of this tragedy, he was instructed to secure the trail for future patrols. In addition, all patrols were decreed to have a First Nations guide accompany them. In 1921, patrols of the trail came to end. In 1964, Dempster died, knowing that the highway, which was still unfinished, was going to be named after him.

The Construction

In 1958, the Canadian government made the decision to build a 671-kilometre two-way road from Dawson City to Inuvik. Oil and gas exploration was booming in the Mackenzie Delta, and the city of Inuvik was under construction. The road was projected as the first-ever overland supply link to southern Canada. The Canadian government also wanted to ensure that the United States, upon discovering huge quantities of oil in the Alaskan region, did not expand its oil fields into Canadian territory. Canada wished to assert its sovereignty over its most northern areas. Business and political circles were buzzing with talk of an oil pipeline that would run parallel to the road, eventually to join another proposed pipeline along the Alaska Highway. Road construction began in January 1959, soon after the Canadian government proclaimed that oil had been discovered in Eagle Plains. The road was necessary for the transportation of equipment, infrastructure, and revenue to and from the oilfields. For political reasons, and due to high costs, construction was halted several times. As a result, building the highway took almost two decades. The intended pipeline was never built. The road was finally completed in 1978, and officially opened on 18 August 1979 at Flat Creek, Yukon. Its design is exceptional due to the tough permafrost conditions that had to be overcome. The road itself sits on top of a gravel pad approximately two metres thick, to insulate the permafrost in the soil beneath. The pad was crucial: without it, the road would sink into the soil. Given the demanding physical conditions of the landscape and the extremely cold temperatures, the engineers had to build the road under excessively harsh circumstances. To make matters worse, very little was known about the region that the proposed highway was to cross, as large sections of the Yukon and Northwest Territories had not yet been mapped.

Exploring the Canadian North: a Dutchman's Perspective

For a person born and raised in the Netherlands, one of the world's most densely populated (approximately 17 million) and smallest countries (it ranks 133rd on the world's country surface area list), it was quite a shock to travel through the world's second largest country with a population of only 34 million. The contrast could hardly have been starker or more overwhelming. Half of Canada's population lives in the big cities along the US-Canadian border, such as Montreal, Ottawa, Toronto, and Vancouver. The other half (as large as the entire Dutch population) is scattered over an area approximately 240 times the size of the Netherlands. Canada's population density, 3.3 inhabitants per square kilometre, is among the lowest in the world. In Canada's "true north" this number is much lower still. Whereas in the Netherlands nearly every square kilometre is overpopulated, overdeveloped, and overregulated, in Canada, the opposite is true: there is an immensity of untouched space, and the sheer vastness of the territory cannot but impress a Dutch traveller, triggering feelings of total freedom, but also of isolation and loneliness.

In August 2005, I experienced these feelings first hand, when my girlfriend and I embarked on the very same journey that Dempster himself had made so many times over a century earlier, from Dawson City to Inuvik. Although one can travel north much faster by plane, we chose to go the slow way, and drive. It turned out to be one of the best choices we ever made, as "driving the Dempster" proved to be an incomparable experience. An enormous challenge, it is, in the words of the Dempster Highway tourist guide, "the thrill of a lifetime." Before tackling the Dempster, we had made several trips through other amazing (and challenging) landscapes worldwide, such as the gorgeous French Alps, the stunning Canadian Rockies along the Icefields Parkway between Banff and Jasper, the impressive plains of Alberta and Saskatchewan, and a number of Australian national parks, such as Alpine National Park. But none of them matched the Dempster. The landscape through which the road cuts is breathtaking. The tundra is covered with colourful Arctic flowers and, as a result of the permafrost, the spruce forest trees in the Eagle Plains area lean in all possible directions. Besides the exciting Arctic tundra, there are striking mountain ranges to see. But above all, the Dempster area is the home of a magnificent variety of animals: Dall's sheep, mountain goats, moose, woodland and barren ground caribou, wolves, wolverines, lynx, fox, grizzly and black bears, not to mention several hundred species of birds, both resident and migratory. Conveniently, in summertime the sun shines 24 hours per day, permitting round-the-clock enjoyment of all the splendours the Dempster has to offer.

We drove to Inuvik in two days, with a short stay in the Eagle Plains Hotel & Service Station. At our starting point in Dawson City, at the Dawson City Visitor Reception Centre, we were offered a "Dempster Highway Passport", with all the "must-see" tourist spots, such as the Tombstone Territorial Park, indicated as checkpoints. At every marked location, a stamp can be collected, ensuring that the visitor who drives, watches, and explores will miss nothing. The instructions provided at the Visitor Centre were given with characteristic Canadian hospitality, efficiency, and generosity: one can be sure to receive the best possible advice, whether asked for or not. Although the trip is a relatively safe one, even for 21st-century travellers, tackling the Dempster is still a challenge; we really felt ourselves to be adventurers exploring the Canadian "New World". This, we felt, was the characteristic Canadian experience: a perfect conjunction of adventure and safety. We saw numerous animals, such as moose, caribou, bald eagles, and bears, in the areas adjacent to the Dempster road. Not all species are friendly to travellers: billions of so-called "black gnats" (very tiny flies that live on animal and human blood) tried to get into our car through the windows; the ones that succeeded feasted on their victims. Furthermore, because the surface of the highway is built of dirt and gravel, the Dempster can be very muddy, which makes for hazardous driving. After rain, the narrow two-way road built on a slope of gravel became so slippery that our car nearly slid off it and onto the spongy tundra. Nevertheless, driving the Dempster is without a doubt the most exciting thing I have ever done. It produces what I have come to think of as the true Canadian feeling: a mixture of loneliness and the conviction that everything in life is possible and that a whole world is waiting to be to explored.

References

Bumsted, J.M. 2003. *A History of the Canadian Peoples*. Second Edition. Don Mills, Ontario: Oxford University Press Canada.

Cunningham, H. 1993. *Insight Guides Canada*. Fourth Edition (revised). Singapore: APA Publications (HK) Höfer Press Pte. Ltd.

Jepson, T. et. al. 1995. *Canada: The Rough Guide*. Second Edition. London: Rough Guides Ltd.

Marchant, G. 1992. *De Canada Reisgids*. Rijswijk: Uitgeverij Elmar B.V., Pacific Rim Press Ltd.

Morrison, W.R., 1985. *Showing the Flag: The Mounted Police and Canadian Sovereignty in the North, 1894-1925*. Vancouver: University of British Columbia Press.

Schulte-Peevers, A., et. al. 2005. *Lonely Planet Canada*, Ninth Edition. Malaysia: Lonely Planet Publications Pty Ltd.

Canada – a travel survival kit. 1994. Fifth Edition. Hong Kong: Lonely Planet Publications, Colorcraft Ltd.

Dorlington Kindersley Travel Guides Canada. 2000. London: Dorlington Kindersley Ltd.

Internet sources

http://en.wikipedia.org/wiki/Dempster_Highway

http://pubs.aina.ucalgary.ca/arctic/Arctic39-2-190.pdf

http://www.dempsterhighway.com/

A Dutch Girl with a First Nations Name:

Studying British Columbia's First Nations Peoples

Irene Salverda

Canada is always on my mind. When I have a tough board meeting at work, my thoughts go back to the meetings I had with First Nations chiefs and Canadian government officials. Cycling the flat Dutch streets, I think back to Vancouver's steep roads, overlooking Burrard Inlet. And when I'm at home with my family, I think about my second home with the First Nations community of Alert Bay, British Columbia.

Irene Salverda

My adventure in Canada began six years ago, in 2004. As a student of Social and Cultural Anthropology at Radboud University, Nijmegen, I developed an interest in Indigenous minorities in western societies. Australia and North America are both examples of western societies with Indigenous minority populations. My particular interest was in the land and resource claims of Indigenous peoples. Canada seemed the perfect country for a research project on this topic. I submitted a proposal to the International Council for Canadian Studies (ICCS), which each year sponsors a number of research projects by foreign students. My proposal was accepted, and I received funding to study land claims of Canada's First Nations peoples. My life-changing experience could begin.

The First Nations Studies Program

On a sunny August afternoon, I landed in Vancouver, British Columbia. I had decided to start my research with a semester of courses at the University of British Columbia (UBC), which offers a First Nations Studies Program. Within this program, students can study Canadian law, ecology, history, and First Nations cultures from an Indigenous perspective.

"Who's indigenous in your country?" was one of the first questions a dark-eyed First Nations classmate asked me. It took a while before I replied: "Me, I think that's me. And my family and friends. We're all indigenous Dutch people." The girl looked puzzled. "Ah. I thought all Europeans were settlers. But I guess you have to come from somewhere, too."

"Who am I?" and "Where do I come from?" are not questions that I often ask myself when I am in the Netherlands. My identity, and the traditions,

Dzawadi, or Knight's Inlet, the traditional place where Kwakwaka'wakw First Nations fish for eulachon.

values, and beliefs that are part of it, seem transparent. They were passed on to me by my grandparents and parents. Some values and beliefs may have changed a little over time, but in essence they're still the same. I support our democratic system, know all about our Dutch history, celebrate *Sinterklaas* on 5 December, and Liberation Day on 5 May.

For Indigenous peoples in Canada, the identity question is more like a puzzle that needs to be put together. After centuries of assimilation politics, conversion to Christianity, and forced education in residential schools, First Nations peoples were left with the questions: "Who are we?" and "Where do we belong?" The Europeans who settled British Columbia caused a rupture in the Indigenous peoples' history of passing on their culture and traditions. Populations decreased dramatically in size and Indigenous practices were prohibited. It was not until the 1980s that First Nations peoples regained the right to practise their own culture and religion. Despite numerous assimilation attempts and repressive politics, First Nations' traditions are still an important part of their everyday lives. But defining a present-day Indigenous identity is more complicated than it seems.

First Nations Peoples in British Columbia

Defining the lands and resources that belong to tribes is part of many First Nations' attempts to establish a modern-day identity. In British Columbia, these land and resource rights are currently negotiated in modern treaty processes. But because defining rights involves two different legal and cultural systems (both First Nations *and* Canadian definitions of rights and ownership), the treaties are often obstructed by communication problems. These intercultural problems caught my attention while studying at UBC in Vancouver.

The Indigenous peoples of British Columbia are in a unique position. British Columbia was one of the last parts of North America to be settled in the 19th century. The settlers seemed to be in a rush. They simply "moved in" and did not take time to negotiate or make treaties with the First Nations peoples who lived there, as was the case in other parts of North America. Indigenous peoples were moved to "reserved land" – reservations that the settlers created and where missionaries undertook to "civilize" them. In the early 1970s, some First Nations in the province started court cases, asserting that their Indigenous rights and titles had never legally been surrendered – and thus still existed. Their claims were successful. In 1982, the Federal Constitution Act was changed to recognize and affirm existing Indigenous rights.

During the 1980s, a modern treaty-making process began. The first band to settle was the Nisga'a tribe, which had been fighting in court since the late 1960s to maintain the land rights it had never surrendered. In 1999, a treaty was established. Many other First Nations in British Columbia began similar treaty-making processes. Currently, about 60 First Nations are involved in claims. Since the Nisga'a success, however, only one additional treaty has been established.

Moving to the Kwakwaka'wakw Reserve

At UBC, I studied the legal aspects of the treaties, but I soon became more interested in studying what was going on in everyday life. In early winter 2005, I travelled to the community of Alert Bay, a village on a small island situated to the northeast of Vancouver Island. Half of the village is "reserve". Alert Bay is home to several of the Kwakwaka'wakw First Nations. The Kwakwaka'wakw consist of roughly twenty different tribes, of which six are struggling in a joint local negotiation process. Shortly after I moved to Alert Bay, I was hired as an intern at the local treaty office. This gave me a unique opportunity to examine legal documents and be present at treaty negotiations between the Canadian government and First Nations chiefs.

The first months I spent on the reserve were hard. I studied at the local museum, ran errands in town, and talked to anyone I met. But somehow, I felt a little ignored. People were friendly, but distant. The weather was cold, grey, and rainy. On windy days, the boat that connected us with Vancouver Island did not run at all. Loneliness turned from a word into a feeling.

Through studying books, artifacts, and maps at the museum, I gained a better understanding of the Kwakwaka'wakw's concerns. Before settlement, the tribes were nomadic, like most tribes in British Columbia. The Kwakwaka'wakw travelled from island to island to hunt, fish, and gather. In wintertime they lived in winter villages where big local feasts and performances – *Potlatches* –

were held. In the spring, summer, and fall, they were on the move, following the runs of fish and the trails of game. Having been a semi-nomadic people, the Kwakwaka'wakw now have a very hard time proving their land claims at the treaty table. The Kwakwaka'wakw used names, songs, and dances to define their territories. Only a village chief knew the specific song or dance of a place and would pass it on to his eldest son. Through trade and performances by chiefs during *Potlatches*, witnessed by community members, property and ownership were recognized. This way, the Kwakwaka'wakw knew which place belonged to which family. Western societies use maps to locate their territories. For them, the Kwakwaka'wakw system of trade and performances for proving ownership could not be used as valid proof in treaty negotiations. So, at the beginning of the treaty process, the governments (both federal and provincial) were ready to acknowledge only about 5% of the territories the Kwakwaka'wakw claimed in the treaty draft.

A brief legal explanation provides further insight into the complications associated with First Nations' treaty processes. In a legal sense, Indigenous rights and treaty rights are different. Indigenous rights are not clearly defined, and hence must be established through the courts on a case-by-case basis. Treaty rights are negotiated, and in modern treaties, rights can be described in detail. The challenge in treaty processes is thus to reach settlement over the Indigenous rights of a tribe. I observed that the Kwakwaka'wakw perceive their rights very differently than the governments do. Some Indigenous views on managing resources include open access to local tribes. This conflicts sharply with the views of the Canadian government as well as with established resource management plans and international agreements. And so continues an unresolved debate as to who has access to what resources, and for which purposes.

Hands-on insight in the Treaty Process

Up to this point in my experience, I had been studying conflicting views only from books. But one windy Tuesday morning, this suddenly changed. At the museum, I had befriended a number of colleagues, one of whom introduced me to a local Indigenous fisherman, George. We talked about treaty processes in general, and the Kwakwaka'wakw process in particular. I explained to George that I would like to know what made the treaty process for Kwakwaka'wakw people so complicated. I knew the facts, but not the feelings. The next day, I received a phone call: "Irene, be at the dock at six a.m. tomorrow morning. I'll take you to a meeting of the Union of B.C. Chiefs. And you'll know, you'll *feel,* why the treaty process is so complicated for us."

Things went quickly from then on. I met many of the local Kwakwaka'wakw Chiefs, who later referred me to their most important elders. Once one of them had agreed to an interview, the others soon followed. I did not speak much during these interviews; instead I listened to stories about living in remote villages on pristine islands, with small families; to stories of hunting, fishing, trapping, and *Potlatching*; to how suddenly, relocation processes began and the elders – who were just children in those days – were taken away to residential schools. Many elders were reluctant to talk about their experiences at these schools. Their stories would usually jump ahead to their life later on, and to how, as insecure young adults, they abused alcohol, and felt depressed and confused about their identity. A short period of hope and glory followed, when the area's fishery became a booming industry. Most of the elders ran boats for about a decade and were able to return to their old practices: fishing, "being out on the ocean." But as the fishery declined, depression, abuse, and grief once again followed. Unemployment levels reached over 85% – and until today have not decreased. The elders trusted me to share their information in a respectful way that would help the treaty process. I decided to include their views on the treaty process in my thesis, but to leave out the more personal stories.

The Challenges of Defining Modern-Day Kwakwaka'wakw Identity

I soon realized that the treaty process was the only way the Kwakwaka'wakw felt their past grievances could be remedied. After Indigenous rights and titles had been affirmed in 1982, First Nations peoples started to feel proud and worthy again. For generations, they had been made to feel embarrassed about their cultural background. Now, people could claim their Indigenous rights and resume traditional cultural practices without risking persecution. The Kwakwaka'wakw treaty process meant a new spark of hope for chiefs and elders – hope to re-establish what had been lost in the past. The chiefs tried to motivate their community members to get involved in the treaty process and to define what Kwakwaka'wakw identity meant to them. This turned out to be a bigger challenge than expected. Indigenous cultures, like Western cultures, had inevitably changed over the years, due to settler influence, globalization, and the modernization of their own culture. The Kwakwaka'wakw were struggling to define their present-day identity. I noticed that some families felt grief over other families' involvement with settlers, years and years ago. There were accusations of falsely claimed territories or traditions of song and dance. And so the goal of establishing a treaty to the benefit of the entire community was impeded by the rise of personal differences. What I saw as the most persistent question while living in Alert Bay was: "What is our present-day shared Aboriginal identity? Who are we?"

I attended some negotiations between Kwakwaka'wakw chiefs and government officials about marine resources. Central to the negotiations was the question: "What can be defined as Indigenous rights in this process?" The first priority of local First Nations with regard to marine resources was to regain control over their traditional fishing territories. Where those territories were located exactly, however, and to what extent their rights could be in place, were issues constantly subject to discussion and debate. Fish stocks in the area were threatened and some of the spawning streams were very vulnerable because of continued forest harvesting practices. The Canadian governments thus wanted to take environmental concerns into account. Even if some fishing rights were granted, they were often overruled by "fisheries closures" – a legal restriction on fishing in a given area.

Out in the Field: Fishing with the Kwakwaka'wakw

During my time in Alert Bay, the annual Kwakwaka'wakw spring fishery for eulachon – a small oily fish – opened. The eulachon fishery is the last fishery in British Columbia that is "open" only to First Nations peoples. To fish, some Kwakwaka'wakw travel up to Knight's Inlet, one of the most stunning areas of British Columbia. At the head of the inlet is the small village of Dzawadi. George, the fisherman whom I had befriended, is a descendant of the tribe that claims the inlet as its territory. He invited me to come along to the annual fishery and experience firsthand how Aboriginal peoples manage their resources. And so I travelled to Dzawadi with an Aboriginal family. We stayed on a small seine boat during the nights, and worked in Dzawadi during the day. There were six Aboriginal families in the village. The women cooked and cleaned while the men prepared the fishing nets. I hiked through beautiful parts of the area and learned a great deal about the territory from the stories of the elders who accompanied me. The lands and rivers had changed dramatically over the years, as fewer people used the traditional areas that are today being affected by increased logging activities and climate change. The effect was clear: we expected runs of thousands of eulachon that year, but while I was there, only several dozen fish passed through the river. We waited, sang, and danced; local legends were passed on from elders to adults and little children. While waiting for the eulachon run, elders taught the younger generation all the cultural practices they remembered. Dzawadi, far from any city, television, or internet connection, seemed like the perfect place to continue passing on cultural practices and traditions. It was wonderful to be able to share in this experience.

New Hope

Just before I left Dzawadi to return to the Netherlands, I was "adopted" by George into his family. I received an Indigenous name, "ma$\underline{x}$'inu$\underline{x}$" (little killer whale) and a crest, the hummingbird. "You'll just have to come back," George said. And so I did. A year later, I spent the summer holidays at my second home. Last summer, in 2009, I visited my "family" again. The treaty negotiations that they are engaged in are still not settled. But when George

Courtesy Irene Salverda

The First Nations crew of a local fishing boat.

picked me up from the airport, there was a sparkle in his eyes. George's extended family – his parents, sisters, and their families – spent an enormous amount of time and effort to rebuild their original home village. Although they are still negotiating the specific rights to their territory, they received federal and provincial government funding for their project by submitting annual proposals for various stages of the building process. The family built a small school, houses, and a lodge for tourists. Among a tangled web of problems, they found a way to look forward to the future.

In the new village, the children are taught two sets of histories: Canadian history and Kwakwaka'wakw history. They learn to perform songs and dances that belong to their families, while at night they watch Canadian ice hockey games. Their English switches fluently to Kwak'wala, the Kwakwaka'wakw language. The treaties may take decades to be settled, but to me it seems as though the new generation of Kwakwaka'wakw children are feeling more at home with who they are in the world.

The Man with Two Hats

Ruben Vroegop

Ruben Vroegop

If they had not lived through it themselves, it would have been wholly inappropriate. But when my grandparents talked between themselves in our southern Limburg dialect about the war years, the discussion frequently derailed into a bizarre game of bragging rights about who had been bombed more often. According to my paternal grandfather, a sad-looking side table served as irrefutable proof that he had lost more than his wife had. A rickety collection of wood and rusty nails was one of the few items salvaged from my grandmother's house after American bombers missed a railway bridge and inadvertently levelled two residential neighbourhoods a mere month before the liberation. According to family lore, my grandfather had already lost everything to a wayward British bomb that had come crashing through the roof earlier in the war.

By the time my grandparents had started practising their English, eating chocolate, and gawking at plain-clothed American officers, a Canadian Private had only just arrived in the war-torn province of Zeeland. A Cameron Highlander attached to the *Régiment de la Chaudière*, he had fought his way through France, was wounded during the Battle of the Scheldt, and would eventually cross into Germany by way of Nijmegen. Among the memories that he would share with his family afterwards, the destitution of the starving population and its overwhelming gratitude during the liberation were to leave an indelible mark on him. Private James Chabot would never meet my quarrelling grandparents. But his granddaughter, who would meet a Dutch exchange student some six decades later, certainly would, thereby adding another storyline to the evolving epic that is the Dutch-Canadian friendship.

Here, in Ottawa, the nation's capital, that historical bond takes on many shapes, including thousands of tulips in springtime and an intriguing sculpture called "The Man with Two Hats". At first glance, it is little more than that – an unremarkable figure of a man, facing eastward, waving two hats. In the Dutch city of Apeldoorn, more than five thousand kilometres and an ocean away, its twin faces west. With every Sunday morning run that leads me past this *bonhomme* in bronze, I become more intrigued with a facial expression that is simultaneously jubilant and melancholic. Perhaps

"The Man with Two Hats" by Dutch artist Henk Visch. Dow's Lake, Ottawa, March 2010.

the cold during these runs makes me slightly delusional or maybe it is the overdose of Gatorade, but the expression reveals a sentiment shared by immigrant farmers, war brides, and simple bureaucrats like yours truly.

Having two hats without wearing either one seems an apt image to describe the cultural dithering of all those hyphenated Canadians who, despite their longing for the fatherland, eventually learn to build a life away from home. Maybe one of the hats should have been a *tuque*. It is all very well to be fashionable, but at minus 30 with a wind chill, you need a decent *tuque*!

First Impressions – and Stereotypes

Seven years ago, a green, inexperienced undergraduate got out of a cab during a snow storm only two blocks away from my current office. The Rideau Canal, an eight-kilometre-long cleared skating rink (enough to make any Frisian green with envy), had opened up the weekend before and I would spend a substantial part of my semester abroad on the ice, dodging hockey sticks, strollers, dogs, runners, hot chocolate stands – basically anything Canadians can take with them or possibly need on the ice.

As the first exchange student from Radboud University, Nijmegen, to attend the University of Ottawa, my objectives were to study hard and explore as much of Canada as I possibly could. Even though I returned to my Dutch stomping grounds five months later with suitcases full of memories, not to mention incredibly tacky souvenirs, I later came to a point that many immigrants will recognize. You can return to your place of origin but you have an undeniable feeling that, in the sage words of Sesame Street, "one of these things just does not belong." The decision to return to Canada for a graduate degree at McGill University in Montreal was easily made. Fortunately for me, the *Cultuurfonds* supported my academic endeavours financially. Although I have always believed that my years in Nijmegen were well spent, the academic quality, financial resources, and intense competition that I would find during my time as a graduate student in Montreal were a real revelation. It was in this vibrant city, the only place besides Maastricht where I have ever truly felt at home, that I stopped pretending my presence abroad was for educational purposes only.

Immigrating is about adapting to new surroundings while adding cultural nuance to preconceived stereotypes. For me, this meant that upon closer inspection, Canucks were not all seven-foot tall, blizzard-defying lumberjacks, nor were they all expert outdoorsmen who single-handedly fought off grizzly bears. Regrettably, I lacked any stereotypes of the *Québécois* at the time, as they are agreeably different: add smoking, *poutine*, and a superior cultural *je ne sais quoi*. As someone once said about English Canada, it could have had British government, American know-how, and French culture, but rather tragically ended up with British know-how, American culture, and French government. *Mon dieu!*

On the happy day that I became a permanent resident, I was asked if I felt up to the task of becoming truly Canadian by buying a pick-up truck and a plaid shirt and ordering a double-double at Tim Horton's drive-through. For those unfamiliar with this cultural phenomenon, Tim Horton's is a coffee chain named after a Canadian hockey player-turned-entrepreneur who built a multi-million dollar coffee empire on a rather basic premise: fast service, low prices, and in my view, questionable quality. Call me a European snob, but a double-double (two creams, two sugars) remains downright vile.

Mind you, stereotypes work both ways and many a Canadian has questioned my claim to Dutch citizenship as I am not blond, lack the telltale guttural Dutch pronunciation when I speak, and grew up *above* sea level. Comic relief aside, we surely have a pleasant, but rather static, stereotypical image of each other. And since it is such a positive image, albeit a comical one, there appears little impetus to change it.

"Trees heeft een Canadees"

If living with the granddaughter of a veteran or seeing the multitude of immaculate Canadian war memorials across Europe did not teach me the significance of military history to Canadian identity, then working alongside the armed forces on a daily basis certainly does. Canada relies heavily on its soldiering past and present to forge its identity as a young nation in an increasingly confusing world. As such, it is no surprise that the lasting bond of friendship between the two countries is a reflection as much of Dutch gratitude to its liberators as of the importance that Canadians place on the liberation as a marker and confirmation of who they are. Small wonder that the two nations get along so well, just like the young Dutch girl, called

Trees, and the Canadian soldier in the Dutch song "*Trees heeft een Canadees*" [Trees has a Canadian], which was so popular in the Netherlands after the liberation.

Walking down the main concourse of the National Defence Headquarters in Ottawa, a walkway lined with paintings depicting the exploits of the Canadian Forces during the First and Second World Wars, one cannot help but feel intimidated. This spot has been my place of work for over two years now and there are days when I still feel as overwhelmed in my cubicle as the day I arrived. It is hard to keep from developing a severe inferiority complex when colleagues your age have flown multi-million-dollar planes around the world, spent weeks on the high seas, or seen several tours in Afghanistan. Fortunately for the troops, Kandahar airfield now boasts a Tim Horton's. And rumour has it that Dutch troops have developed quite a liking for the sickly-sweet iced cappuccino.

Last summer, I had the pleasure of visiting several military bases in eastern Canada. Apart from nearly cracking my skull in the back of an armoured vehicle in Gagetown, New Brunswick, and almost being thrown overboard in Halifax harbour during a visit with the Navy, and climbing into the cockpit of a CF-18 in Chicoutimi, Quebec, the people I met also made a lasting impression. Most of them invariably associate modern-day Holland with the International Four Days Marches Nijmegen and the euphoric response their uniforms still incite from the very start to the last metres on *Via Gladiola*. The competition to be part of the Canadian Forces contingent is fiercer every year, and recruitment posters highlight the memorable bonding, or more accurately, reconnecting, between Dutch civilians and Canadian soldiers. Apart from such festive events, it remains hard to grasp the possibility that the driven and committed Corporal you talk to one day could be the one mourned during a moment of silence at headquarters another day.

For many of us, it has always been painless and routine to support human rights, freedom, and democracy from the comfort of our home or academic ivory tower. I never fully understood the drive of these young soldiers to sit in the back of an infernally hot and claustrophobic armoured vehicle, fighting for a faraway land, fully aware of the stakes. But talk with any of them for a couple of minutes, and you will catch a glimpse of previous generations who crossed an ocean over 65 years ago to fight for a country that most of them did not even have stereotypical notions about. Without commenting on the rationale or viability of the current mission in Afghanistan, I have a deep respect and lasting sympathy for every single soldier, as do those who line "the highway of heroes" when another fallen son or daughter comes home. Regrettably, in the current media-hyped environment, the level of support for the individual soldier sometimes appears to depend on the palatability of the mission in the political arena.

Courtesy Ruben Vroegop

The National War Memorial (centre) and the Peace Tower (right) in downtown Ottawa, May 2009.

The Good Old Hockey Game

Apart from military history, a less serious, but perhaps equally important aspect that infuses Canadian society with a sense of place, meaning, and community is its fanatical, near-religious devotion to the sport of hockey, always "ice" hockey, not "field" hockey. Dutch readers may consider a comparison here with *koning voetbal* [Dutch soccer] in the Netherlands, but in all honesty, there is no comparing the two sports. There are hockey talk shows in the heat of summer, hockey sticks outnumber the resident population at least two to one, and number "99" (hockey star Wayne Gretzky's number) is arguably bigger in Canada than number "14" (of legendary soccer player Johan Cruijff) is in the Netherlands.

While mingling in the hurricane of sticks and gear too big for the small bodies that define "Timbit" minor hockey (another reference to Tim Horton's), young Canadians learn the moral code of a game that applies to life both on and off the rink. The sport draws the country closer together as it is one of the few passions that Canadians truly share, from Newfoundland to British Columbia and, should you have already discussed the rain or fog in either province, it is a sure starter for small talk. Just make sure to remind them that the *Canadiens de Montréal* have won 24 Stanley Cups.

On the rink, Canucks loathe unsportsmanlike conduct and whining to the referee while revelling in hard work, toothless grins, and fair fights. They are polite to a point, and usually remove their helmets before engaging an opponent in a fight so as not to cut his hand (although noses may be broken). They would much rather have 16 stitches and lose the game in a blow-out than win by diving for a penalty shot. Needless to say that until this changes, Canada will maintain its abysmal track record at soccer.

There is no denying the stereotype that Canadians value being polite. They also like to be not-American and will scoff at the United States throwing its weight around on the global playground, even though it is not necessarily its insolence that Canadians take offence to so much as the unbridled confidence about its "manifest destiny". After all, when you are "sleeping with an elephant", as Prime Minister Trudeau once defined the Canadian-American relationship, any victory that sets you apart can be of great importance. Therefore, beating the Americans at hockey seems more important than a WTO ruling on the softwood lumber dispute. Prime Minister Harper could not have been happier than when he won a bet with President Obama over the outcome of the 2010 Olympic men's hockey final and received the wager delivered to his doorstep – a case of Molson Canadian beer (which, again, is undrinkable).

One Last Stereotype

Fortunately, stereotypes obscure as much as they reveal and, as stated before, the Dutch perspective on all things Canadian hides a considerable part of this humongous country and its people. With the legacy of the Second World War soon to become the exclusive domain of historians, and the increasingly globalized world, we may over time perhaps develop a more holistic understanding of each other. Future Dutch immigrants who will sport a second hat one day will find, just as I did, that Canada is less pristine and less perfect than we at times were led to believe. This country has problems like any other, and immigrating, ironically, also means realizing just how blessed a place such as the Netherlands truly is. A Canadian colleague once told me that if Dutch *stroopwafels* [waffle-shaped treacle cookies] were representative of my country, she would file for immigration the same day.

Despite endured hardships over the years, the Dutch immigrant community has thrived in Canada like few others. Immigrant farmers and war brides have earned the Dutch a reputation for being fair, straight-talking, hard workers. Our integration into the Canadian mosaic is so seamless and inconspicuous that were it not for our wholly unpronounceable last names, we would simply vanish altogether. Still, the relative invisibility of the Dutch in Canada has been more a matter of choice than chance, and we can count ourselves fortunate to be in such an enduring position of luxury.

Commemorating the 65th anniversary of the liberation of the Netherlands by Canadian troops means celebrating our friendship in all its historical realities and quaint subjective stereotypes. It means commemorating the Canadian soldiers, war brides, and all those children with two hats who came out of one of the darkest episodes in our shared history to help build what is arguably one of the best countries in the world. But then again, modesty is just another stereotypically Canadian trait. And they know how to make love in a canoe too!

Introduction

The Netherlands Centre for Canadian Studies

Jeanette den Toonder
University of Groningen

The Centre, founded in 1988 at the University of Groningen, is the only Canadian Studies Centre in the Netherlands. Its objective is the promotion of education and research related to different aspects of Canada. Through its members, a large number of disciplines is represented: Literature, Literary Translation, Linguistics, Communication Studies, American Studies, Arctic Studies, Anthropology, History, Political Science, Geography, Law, Management and Organization. The contribution of these varied fields of study offers the possibility of interdisciplinary research.

Interdisciplinarity has been an essential element of a large number of international conferences organized by the Centre, on topics related to the cultural space and geography of Canada, Mexico, and the United States ("Crossing Cultures: Travel and the Frontiers of North-American Identity", May 2003), or focusing on an interdisciplinary approach to representations of space within Canada ("Re-exploring Canadian Space / Redécouvrir l'espace canadien," November 2008). Two of the Centre's major francophone conferences, in 2001 and 2007, examined the interrelation of space and gender in Quebec literature ("*Espace et sexuation dans la littérature québécoise*", May 2001) and presented the broader scope of francophone literature in Canada today (*Écritures de l'intime dans la littérature francophone du Canada*, April 2007). The proceedings of these conferences have been published in Canada and the Netherlands.

Within the University of Groningen, the Centre for Canadian Studies has established a special collaboration with the Arctic Centre. Sharing their interest in Inuit cultures, climate change, and ecology, the two Centres have organized workshops on the dynamics of and changes in Arctic Canada.

Research interests at the Centre have paid special attention to the literatures of Quebec and French-Canada. Many scholars and authors have been invited to give lectures on *Québécois* and French-Canadian literary perspectives on the North American continent. The Centre's members have published widely on travel writing, *écriture migrante*, and space and identity. To date, two volumes on these topics have been published: *Romans de la route et voyages identitaires* (eds. Jean Morency, Jaap Lintvelt, Jeanette den Toonder, 2006) and *Voix du temps et de l'espace* (ed. Jeanette den Toonder, 2007). Of particular interest is the Centre's collaborative project with the *Université de Moncton,* New Brunswick, focusing on Acadian literature and culture.

In addition to numerous academic articles published over the years by its members in the fields of language, translation, literature, politics, history, law, and geography, the Centre's recent publications include Ph.D. theses by Kurt Niquidet, *Essays on the Economics of British Columbian Timber Policy* (Groningen, 2007), and Kim van Dam, *A Place called Nunavut. Multiple identities for a new region* (Groningen, 2008). The documentary, *A Forest for the Future* (2009), on the struggle for preservation of the Great Bear Rainforest, was produced by Bettina van Hoven and Annemieke Logtmeijer as a part of a teaching pack for use in Dutch secondary schools and for first year Geography students. Supported by the Banff International Literary Translation Centre, Pauline Sarkar translated the Quebec writer Anne Hébert's novel, *Un habit de lumière,* into Dutch, *Klatergoud* (Barkhuis Publishers, Groningen, 2009).

The Centre offers a Minor in Canadian Studies, focusing on the study of Canada's multicultural society from different disciplinary and methodological angles. Canadian guest lecturers participate in these courses. Currently, the program proposes an introduction to the history of multicultural Canada and the country's current political situation, as well as courses on the geographical and multicultural demographic characteristics of Canada, and on the study of literature and culture in its multicultural contexts in Canada and Quebec.

The Centre attaches great importance to international cooperation and to actively engaging students in its activities. To this end, cooperation agreements have been concluded with seven Canadian universities (anglophone and francophone) that participate in student exchanges. Yearly, approximately 50 students (Canadian and Dutch) participate in these exchange programs.

In early 2010, a student platform was created, sponsored by the TD Waterhouse Bank, to enable students to organize activities exploring Canada's multifaceted character. This has generated even greater interest in Canadian society and culture amongst the university's student population. Two events focusing on current topics have already been organized: a lecture evening presenting different perspectives on the Olympic Games in Vancouver, and a debate comparing and contrasting ideas on governance in Canada and the Netherlands.

The importance of the Centre with regard to academic relationships between Canada and the Netherlands was recognized and emphasized in 1996 during the visit to the Netherlands by then Governor General of Canada, H.E. Roméo LeBlanc, accompanied by Her Majesty Queen Beatrix. They visited the University of Groningen, where they attended a presentation on the exchange program with Canadian universities. On 7 May 2005, Their Excellencies, The Right Honourable Adrienne Clarkson, Governor General of Canada, and Mr. John Ralston Saul visited the University of Groningen to attend a presentation of the Canadian Studies Centre. As the visit took place within the framework of the 60th anniversary of Dutch liberation in 1944-45, the Centre was pleased to welcome Canadian veterans among its guests.

Close contacts have been established with the Canadian Embassy in the Netherlands, the *Délégation générale du Québec* in Brussels, the International Council for Canadian Studies (Ottawa), and the Ministry of Foreign Affairs (The Hague). The Centre is supported by the Canadian Government and represented by the Canadian Embassy and the Association for Canadian Studies in the Netherlands.

Representing the Centre in this volume are essays by two of its students, Emma Kutka and Marijn van Vliet, who are pursuing their Bachelor's degrees at the University of Groningen. Emma Kutka is a Canadian exchange student from Queen's University in Kingston, Ontario, where she studies Political Science. During her stay in Groningen, she has developed a special interest in the political situation in the Netherlands and actively engages in events promoting Canadian Studies in this country. Marijn van Vliet has been an exchange student as well, having spent a semester at *Université Laval* in Quebec City, Canada, where he gained further insight into the relationship between Canada and the Netherlands. Marijn is an active member of the Centre's student platform and participates in information evenings organized by the university and the Faculty of Arts, advising interested students on the exchange programs between the University of Groningen and its Canadian partner universities. Because of their cross-cultural interests, active participation in the Centre's activities, and familiarity with both countries, these students have been chosen to present their views on the relations between Canada and the Netherlands.

National Identity:
Canada's Model of Multiculturalism

Emma Kutka

As a Canadian student living and studying in the Netherlands, I am occasionally asked: "What is typically Canadian?" I always have a difficult time giving a straight answer, because I myself do not know what is typical for all Canadians. Canadian identity cannot be defined the same way Dutch identity can. What is typically Dutch seems to me to be easier to articulate. Like many European countries, the Netherlands' national identity is the outcome of a shared history, language, heritage, religion, and culture. On a number of counts, Canada's national identity cannot compare to that of the Netherlands. In the first instance, Canadian history is short in comparison to Dutch history. Secondly, with the exception of Canada's Native peoples, we are a country settled almost entirely by immigrants. Added to our French-English biculturalism, this means that we do not have a common heritage, religion, culture, and language. Other factors that make it difficult to define a shared Canadian national identity include the vastness of Canadian geography and Canadian multiculturalism. Canada is distinct in its approach to multiculturalism, which encompasses French-English biculturalism and cultural pluralism. The Netherlands is currently facing the increased ethnic and cultural diversity of a globalized world. Dutch national identity is at a juncture because of the perceived threat of multiculturalism. The Netherlands needs to make changes in order to manage multiculturalism, immigration, and integration within the Dutch culture. Canada offers an example of how to maintain, through multicultural policy, national identity in a country of many cultures.

Canadian Immigration

Canada's multicultural identity stems from a history of immigration. The Dutch were among the many European immigrants to Canada, settling first in the west where there were good opportunities for work and later in the more urban areas of central Canada. According to figures in *The Canadian Encyclopedia*, approximately 25,000 Dutch came to Canada, specifically to Toronto and the surrounding areas, between World War I and the 1930s. The last large influx of Dutch immigrants came after World War II. Many were war brides, while others left a war-weary Europe to start a new life in

Emma Kutka

Canada. According to Statistics Canada, there are currently 111,990 Dutch immigrants living in Canada, and 1,035,965 Canadians of Dutch descent (2006).

Since the 1970s, Canada has experienced increased immigration from Asia, Africa, Latin America, and the Caribbean, and less from Europe. In her 1992 study, *Strangers at our Gates*, Valerie Knowles argues that the Immigration Act of 1976, which is the basis of Canada's modern immigration policy, created a non-discriminatory immigration policy eliminating racial and geographical discrimination. Non-Europeans were able to immigrate to Canada more easily, creating a country of more visible minorities, as well as a need to manage diversity.

Immigration remains important in Canada. In 2008, 247,243 people immigrated to Canada (Government of Canada, 2009). I myself am the product of recent immigration. My mother immigrated to Canada from Ireland in the 1960s, and my father's parents emigrated from Lithuania in the 1940s. I was born in Canada and have lived there most of my life. Although I am Canadian, it is normal for me to consider myself Irish and Lithuanian as well, especially when talking with fellow Canadians about our backgrounds. Multiculturalism is about acknowledging the differences between cultural groups, races, and ethnicities, and trying to maintain them. People feel pride when discussing their heritage and it is not generally considered racist or discriminatory in Canada to talk about different ethnic backgrounds.

Canadian Multiculturalism

What does a Canadian look like? This question became almost impossible to answer after the 1970s, especially in the metropolitan areas of Toronto, Vancouver, Calgary, and Montreal. Canada was quickly becoming an ethnically plural country, Trudeau's 1971 multiculturalism policy having aimed to promote diversity and prevent racism (Knowles, 1992). The policy advocated a culturally plural society and the concept of cultural pluralism as a way to manage its diversity. This pluralism is often referred to as a "cultural mosaic", meaning many different cultures, living side by side in harmony. Tolerance, rather than assimilation, was promoted. The policy also encouraged and assisted immigrants to learn at least one of the official languages.

In 1982, multiculturalism was institutionalized in the Canadian Charter of Rights and Freedoms, recognizing the need to preserve cultural heritage and to treat all people equally under the law, "without discrimination based on race, national or ethnic origin, colour, religion, sex, age, or mental or physical disability" (Government of Canada, 1982). The Multiculturalism Act came into effect in 1988, making Canada the first country in the world to

Canadians celebrating in Vancouver after the Canadian men's hockey team won gold at the Vancouver 2010 Olympics.

Courtesy Jan Gates.

pass a law on national multiculturalism (Government of Canada, 2006). The Act gave the responsibility of racial and cultural equity to the legal system and demanded that government, at many levels and departments, support Canada's multiculturalism. The public was also expected to support and embrace multiculturalism.

Some of Canada's majority population, as well as some minority groups, have argued against Canadian multiculturalism. Multiculturalism, they maintain, deteriorates Canadian identity and undermines Canadian unity because it emphasizes difference instead of promoting a strong collective identity. It also creates racism because of the emphasis on cultural difference. This argument is heard in the Netherlands today, as well as in the United States, from those who favour assimilation as a means of managing immigration and diversity.

Canadian multiculturalism is constantly developing and presenting itself to the world. The recent 2010 Winter Olympics in Vancouver demonstrated how diverse and proud Canadians are, and how united we are as a nation. Scholars like Reza Nakhaie have shown that minorities in Canada have a "warm feeling" towards the country, as well as towards their ethnic background (Nakhaie, 2006). The Olympics also paid particular attention to Canada's Aboriginal peoples, whose relationship with the government, both in the past and in the present, remains an area where work needs to be done.

Canada's unparalleled response to the devastating January 2010 earthquake in Haiti was – and still is – unwavering. Canada has a humanitarian role in the world but that is not the only reason for the great support shown for

Haiti. In 2001, 82,000 people living in Canada were of Haitian origin, many in Quebec (Government of Canada, 2007). Canada has created special immigration policies for Haitians who have Canadian family members. The federal government has worked to accelerate the adoption process of Haitian children. When disaster struck Haiti at the outset of 2010, Canadian troops were quickly deployed to the island. Canadians have donated generous amounts of time and money, which not only supports Haiti, but also shows support for Haitians in Canada.

Canada's Governor General, Michaëlle Jean, is Haitian-Canadian. Her 2010 Speech from the Throne emphasized the traits that make us proud as Canadians, including our aid for Haiti and our success at the Olympics. "To be Canadian," she stated, "is to show the world that people drawn from every nation can live in harmony" (2010). Canada is an example of multiculturalism for the world.

Dutch Multiculturalism

The Netherlands has historically been seen as a homogenous population with one predominant culture. Dutch identity was not about diversity and pluralism, and there was no need to include these issues as topics for discussion. According to current Statistics Netherlands, however, 1,859,315 citizens of the Netherlands have a non-Western background (2010); they were either born outside the Netherlands in a non-Western country, or one or both of their parents were born outside the Netherlands in a non-Western country. The increase in immigration, specifically of visible minorities, in the last 50 years has complicated Dutch identity.

Studies have shown that most of the immigrants who came to the Netherlands during the past 50 years were from former Dutch colonies (Indonesia, Surinam, and the Dutch Antilles), or from southern Europe, Turkey, or Morocco, or from former Eastern Bloc countries (Schalk-Soekar et. al., 2004). Because of this influx of diversity, the Netherlands adopted a policy of multiculturalism in the 1980s. Like Canada's policy, it sought to promote cultural diversity, respect, equal rights, and an equal voice for all people.

The early approach to multiculturalism in the Netherlands saw immigrant minorities in separate "pillar" groups. It was argued that minority groups could live separately and eventually assimilate into Dutch society, leaving behind their own cultures when they were ready (Verheul, 2009). This approach was unsuccessful in the Netherlands. Immigrants did not assimilate, and there was no social emancipation. Many became part of an underclass of Dutch society. The failure of multiculturalism prior to 2000 in the Netherlands has been seen as a threat to national order and to the quality of Dutch life. The country would like to improve the livelihoods of minority immigrants by promoting assimilation into Dutch society, but this has become a topic for debate. In the case of the Netherlands' Muslim population, for example, neo-conservatives claim that Islamic culture and values conflict with those of Dutch culture. Where the Dutch value individualism and social symmetry, they argue, Islam favours the collective and hierarchy. Neo-conservatives maintain that Islam does not have a place in the Netherlands and that Muslim immigrants must fully integrate into Dutch society (Verheul, 2009). Only assimilation, they insist, will prevent racism, because it does not emphasize the differences between cultures.

How do immigrants and minorities affect Dutch identity? The homogenous Dutch identity – which predominated until the influx of immigration to the Netherlands – is changing. The people of the Netherlands no longer all share a common language, culture, heritage, religion, and history. What is typically Dutch is becoming more difficult to define because not all minorities are assimilating into Dutch society.

The threat to Dutch identity has been an important topic in the Netherlands. In 2007, for example, the Crown Prince's wife, Princess Máxima, commented that the Dutch are too diverse to rely on stereotypes to define their identity. This caused a great deal of reaction, especially from those who feel that Dutch identity does exist and can be defined. The issue is not whether Dutch identity exists or not, however, but how the increase of immigrants and minorities in the Netherlands fits in with Dutch identity. The Canadian model of multiculturalism offers an example of how different cultures can be part of a national identity. Canadian multiculturalism obliges the legal system to promote diversity and cultural pluralism, and has public support.

Public support for multiculturalism in the Netherlands is declining. The Freedom Party of the Netherlands and its far-right leader, Geert Wilders, have made a platform of anti-immigration and anti-Islamic attitudes, and they are gaining popular support. If the collapse of the Dutch coalition cabinet in February 2010 was caused by the resignation from the Cabinet by the Labour Party, who did not want to extend the Netherlands' Afghanistan mission, the political crisis also expressed tensions between the political parties with regard to questions of nationalism and identity. Intercultural relations scholars such as Saskia Schalk-Soekar argue that, in order to promote multicultural support from the majority, there needs to be increased contact and understanding between majority and minority groups (Schalk-Soeka et. al., 2004). This will reduce racism and the fear that immigrants and multiculturalism are threats to Dutch identity.

The Netherlands and Canada have a great deal in common, including a commitment to international human rights protection. Anti-immigration attitudes and racism indicate that not all domestic human rights are protected in the Netherlands. There is need for a multiculturalism policy that promotes tolerance and cultural diversity at the legal and institutionalized levels,

Courtesy Anke Teunissen

as well as at the public level. Multiculturalism is not a threat to national identity, for a country's identity can encompass many cultures, religions, and ethnicities, and still be a united country.

Before I came to the Netherlands I had an image of what was typically Dutch. That image included tall blond people on bicycles, wearing wooden shoes, and eating cheese sandwiches. I quickly learned that such traits are only symbols of the Netherlands. What it means to be Dutch, and what identifies a citizen of the Netherlands, cannot be so easily pinpointed. I now know that in the Netherlands, people are hardworking and friendly, that they care for the well-being of others, and that they are not afraid to tell you what they think. Now when I am asked, "What is typically Canadian?" I reply that, like the Dutch, we care about others and work hard to help out the less fortunate, that we are friendly, and proud to be a country of many cultures.

References

Ganzevoort, Herman. "Dutch." *The Canadian Encyclopedia*. Retrieved from the web 8 March 2010.

Government of Canada. 1982. *Canadian Charter of Rights and Freedoms.*

Government of Canada. 2006. *Canadian Multiculturalism*. Library of Parliament. 16 March 2006. Retrieved 8 March 2010 from http://www.parl.gc.ca/information/library/PRBpubs/936-e.htm#1theincipient

Government of Canada. 2006. *Population by ethnic origins, by province and territory (2006 Census)*. Statistics Canada. Retrieved 5 March 2010 from http://www40.statcan.gc.ca/l01/cst01/demo26a-eng.htm

Government of Canada. 2007. *The Haitian Community in Canada.* Statistics Canada. 28 August 2007. Retrieved 5 March 2010 from http://www.statcan.gc.ca/pub/89-621-x/89-621-x2007011-eng.htm

Government of Canada. 2009. *Facts and figures 2008 – Immigration overview: Permanent and temporary residents.* Citizenship and Immigration Canada. 28 August 2009. Retrieved 8 March 2010 from http://www.cic.gc.ca/English/resources/statistics/facts2008/permanent/01.asp

Government of the Netherlands. 2010. *Population; generation, sex, age and origin*. Statistics Netherlands. 13 March 2010. Retrieved from the web 17 March 2010.

Jean, Michaëlle. 2010. *Speech from the Throne*. Government of Canada. Canadian Parliament, Ottawa, Canada. Retrieved from the web 11 March 2010.

Knowles, Valerie. 1992. *Strangers at our Gates: Canadian Immigration and Immigration Policy, 1540-1990*. Toronto: Dundurn Press Ltd.

Nakhaie, M Reza. 2006. "Contemporary Realities and Future Visions: Enhancing Multiculturalism in Canada." *Canadian Ethnic Studies* 38.1: 149-158.

Schalk-Soekar, Saskia R.G., Fons J.R. van de Vijer and Mariette Hoogsteder. 2004. "Attitudes Toward Multiculturalism of Immigrants and Majority Members in the Netherlands." *International Journal of Intercultural Relations* 28: 533-550. Retrieved from the web 8 March 2010.

Verheul, Jaap. 2009. " How could this have happened in Holland?" *American Multiculturalism after 9/11: Transatlantic Perspectives*. Eds. Ruben, Derek and Jaap Verheul. Amsterdam: Amsterdam University Press. 191-206.

"When They Ask Who Freed Us..."

Pro Amicis Mortui Amicis Vivimus

"We live in the hearts of friends for whom we died."

Marijn van Vliet

Marijn van Vliet

As we celebrate the 65th anniversary of the liberation of the Netherlands, we remember Canada's important contribution, which created a close bond between the peoples of the two countries. This bond continues to this day, as I myself have experienced. In the winter of 2009, I had the privilege of going to Canada and spending a semester at the *Université Laval* in Quebec City. During my time there, I was asked to offer my perspective, as the only European in class, on an essay written by Salman Rushdie, entitled "American Culture is not the Enemy" (Rushdie, 1999). In this essay, Rushdie discusses the resistance to American culture and foreign policy on the part of some Europeans, which he perceives as a lack of gratitude to their liberators. This statement touched me profoundly. Perhaps it was because Rushdie saw the United States as the sole liberating force of Western Europe, whereas my home town, Groningen, and a large part of my country, the Netherlands, were liberated by Canadian soldiers. Thus, as a Dutchman, my gratitude is primarily to Canada. Perhaps, too, it was the thought of my grandfather, forced into hiding to escape being ordered to work in a German factory, who was liberated by Canadian soldiers, to whom he owed his life. How could his feelings of gratitude be questioned?

Rushdie, a British-Indian novelist born in Bombay and educated in the United Kingdom, became an American citizen after the Second World War. Where, I wondered, does his claim about gratitude come from? Is he right in suggesting that Europeans should express their gratitude in more substantive ways, as opposed to primarily symbolic ways? Should the Dutch show more gratitude to Canada than they do now, and what form would more substantive gratitude take? Might it involve, following Rushdie's argument, more support for Canadian foreign policy and culture? Does gratitude extend to supporting another country's foreign policy?

These questions raise the issue of the significance of commemorating past events for the present and the future, including the events surrounding the liberation. In this essay, I will consider Rushdie's statements about gratitude from a Dutch perspective. Because the Netherlands was liberated primarily by Canadians, I will focus on the Dutch-Canadian relationship, in the hope

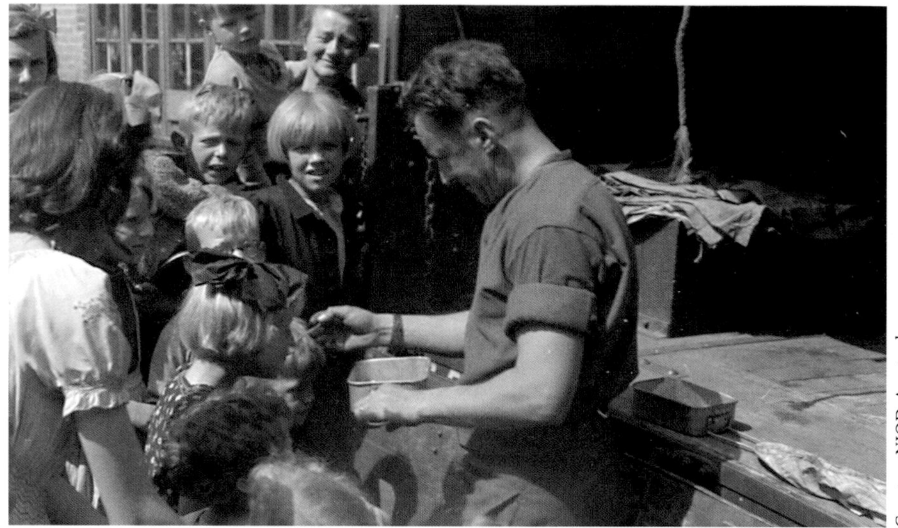

A Canadian soldier distributing food to Dutch children.

Courtesy NIOD, Amsterdam.

that my comments might provide some insight into the ways the Dutch experienced liberation at the end of the Second World War, and the ways they remember the sacrifices that were made for their freedom. In addition, by commenting on Rushdie's controversial remarks, I hope to explain why the Dutch still commemorate liberation by the Canadians and the relevance of this in looking to the future.

The role that Canada played in liberating the Netherlands has had a very positive effect on the relationship between the two countries. At the outset of the war, Canada welcomed Princess Juliana and her two daughters, Beatrix and Irene, after they were forced to flee the Netherlands. Ottawa would become their home for the next few years. It also became the birthplace of Princess Margriet, strengthening the ties between the Dutch Royal family and Canada. The ties would become stronger still as a result of Canada's role in the liberation of Holland.

In the winter of 1945, only the southern part of the Netherlands had been liberated; most of the country was still under German occupation. The final winter of the war was particularly difficult for the Dutch. It was a very cold, harsh winter and the supply of coal from the south of the country was cut off. So, too, were food supplies. People had to become very resourceful in obtaining fuel and food. The wooden parts of the tram rails in Amsterdam, for example, were all used as fuel for warmth or cooking. Food shortages in the city led people on long, difficult treks to the countryside in the hope of trading valuables for food. Men, women, and children, some of them barefoot, walked for miles through the blistering cold. Some 20,000 people lost their lives during that winter. Near its end, Canada brokered an agreement with Germany to allow coordinated airdrops of food and supplies by the Allied Forces. The Royal Canadian Air Force participated in these mercy missions.

For the Dutch, this was their first encounter with Canadians, and many were inspired to paint "Thank You, Canadians!" on their rooftops as a way of showing their appreciation.

With the liberation of northern Holland in the spring of 1945, the Dutch came to know their liberators even better. During the five years of occupation, many Dutch Jews had been mistreated and murdered, family members had been taken away to work in German factories and labour camps, children had seen death, and citizens had lost their freedom. When the Canadians arrived in their jeeps, with chocolates and cigarettes, they were immediately welcomed into the hearts of many Hollanders. One can only imagine the emotion of being freed from oppression after so many years, of having no more fear of being taken away, or tortured, or killed. Families could be reunited. People who were in hiding, like my grandfather, could once again lead the lives they wanted to live.

In 1946, Anneke Klein Klouwenberg, a little girl living in Deventer, wrote a letter to all Canadian soldiers who had served in the Netherlands. Published in *The Hamilton Spectator* in Canada, it offers a glimpse into the emotion of liberation. Anneke wrote:

> When you [Canadian soldiers] on a, for us, historical day, entered the capital of our country, from all sides the boys and girls jumped on your jeeps, then you found a nation of grateful and moved people, who hardly knew their happiness. First you didn't understand the tears you saw in many eyes and you couldn't understand that, because you didn't know the sufferings from which thousands of men, women and children went to rack and ruin and that we all, when you got acquainted withus, bore in despair.

Those who lived through the war and experienced the liberation, who owe their lives to their liberators, do not forget what was done for them. They are grateful and want to keep the memory of the brave young Canadians alive to pass their story on to the next generation. As Anneke Klein Klouwenberg wrote: "our grandchildren will ask us who liberated us and then we will say, many brave boys with caps on their heads; we shall tell them all much, and much more than that Montreal and Ottawa are two big cities in Canada."

The desire to remember has evolved into a national commemoration each year on 4 May, when the whole country observes two minutes of silence to remember all who lost their lives during the Second World War. This is followed by a day of celebration to commemorate the freedom that we enjoy today. The streets are lined with people eager to catch a glimpse of the veterans who are invited to be part of the celebration.

But is this enough? In his 1999 essay, Rushdie links the Second World War to more recent events, such as the bombing of Iraq and the capture of the Kurdish leader Abdullah Öcalan, implying that European failure to support these acts constitutes a lack of gratitude on the part of Europeans to their liberators at the end of the Second World War. Is it the case, then, as discussed above, that the Dutch should show more substantive gratitude to Canada, in particular by supporting its foreign policy? This may at first seem a valid question, if viewed as follows: we sacrificed for your freedom during the Second World War; how about helping us out now? This, however, would have serious consequences for Dutch foreign policy. It would mean taking Canada's interest into consideration on every policy decision made by the Netherlands. Is that the kind of gratitude that Rushdie has in mind? In my opinion, blindly following another country's foreign policy is not a sign of gratitude. It is a sign of compliance. The Canadian soldiers who freed the Netherlands did so to free the Dutch. Any obligation to follow the foreign policy of its liberator, as Rushdie suggests, would severely limit that freedom, which runs counter to the very principle of liberation. With the freedom of liberation comes the freedom for a country to maintain its own policies – and its own culture. Differences in culture should be respected. It was, after all, partly to protect Dutch culture that those brave young Canadians sacrificed their lives.

Should Canada's freedom ever be threatened, then the Dutch would surely do anything we could to help. That is the kind of relationship that the events surrounding the liberation have created. True friendship means providing support, but also advice and criticism when appropriate. The Dutch show their gratitude to Canadians not in the way Rushdie suggests, but by honouring the veterans, their families, and their fallen friends. They were the ones who risked their lives for Holland in 1944-45; they were the ones who made sacrifices for our freedom; and so they are the ones who deserve our gratitude. Ask any veteran who comes to Holland to commemorate the liberation; he will tell you that Canadians are deeply moved by the way they are welcomed. The Dutch are proud to show their gratitude to their liberators, and for as long as veterans are able to come to Holland, they can expect a warm reception. In Lance Goddard's book, *Canada and the Liberation of the Netherlands* (2005), Elly Dull writes about her experience of the 50th anniversary of the liberation. It sums up Dutch sentiment well:

> There were planeloads of veterans going over; I think six thousand in total plus their care givers. We went in April and I made sure that my children were there because they were really brought up with this story, and I remember being moved, and there were some veterans ahead of me in Schiphol airport and as they went through the passport check the veteran presented his passport and the customs official said, "Sir, we didn't ask for your passport when you entered here fifty years ago, and we don't ask for it now. Please be welcome."

In commemorating the 65th anniversary of the liberation, the Dutch not only look back and honour those who sacrificed their lives for our liberty; we also look forward to seeing how we can pass along the torch of freedom. The day will come when we will no longer have the honour of welcoming veterans to our country. Should we then stop remembering the events of the past? No! Every day, the newspapers offer painful proof that what has come to pass for us has not come to pass for all in the world. This should remind us, and generations to come, that freedom is not a given. It has taken great sacrifice from a great generation to make it possible, and with that sacrifice comes a great duty – the duty to remember and to protect. This is why it is so important to keep commemorating the liberation and the freedom that it brought. It takes the commitment of every generation to hold the torch high. We must ask what we can do to protect our freedom, while trying to help others protect theirs. As Robert F. Kennedy put it, in a speech addressed to the entire world: "each time a man stands for an ideal, or acts to improve the lot of others, or strikes out against injustice, he sends forth a tiny ripple of hope, and crossing each other from a million different centres of energy and daring, those ripples build a current which can sweep down the mightiest walls of oppression and resistance" (1966).

To shape the future, however, we must study the past. It is clear that Canada played a significant role in the history of our country; we Dutch enjoy a special relationship with Canadians because of this. I personally have benefited from this great bond and I will never forget the kind and generous spirit of the Canadians I met, just as the bravery and generosity of the Canadian people during our time of need will not be forgotten by the Dutch. As Anneke Klein Klouwenberg, the little girl from Deventer, wrote to soldiers in Canada in 1946: "maybe you will see a tear in the eyes of your mother, your wife, your girl or your sister, but don't forget that a tear is a smile of the heart, and that same heart is beating in the small low-lying country near the sea, Holland, that will set down your name in the chronicles of history."

References

Goddard, Lance. 2005. *Canada and the Liberation of the Netherlands, May 1945.* Toronto: Dundurn Group.

Kennedy, Robert. 1966. "Day of Affirmation" speech given at the University of Capetown, Capetown, South Africa, 6 June 1966. http://www.jfklibrary.org/Historical+Resources/Archives/Reference+Desk/Speeches/RFK/Day+of+Affirmation+Address+News+Release.htm

Klein Klouwenberg, Anneke. 1946. "When They Ask Who Freed Us..." *The Hamilton Spectator*, 25 March 1946.

Rushdie, Salman. 1999. "American Culture is not the Enemy." in *The Harbrace Reader for Canadians.* Joanne Buckley (2001). Toronto: Thomson Nelson. 335-337.

Notes on Contributors

Hans Bak, Ph.D. is professor of American Literature at Radboud University, Nijmegen, NL. His reseach interests include contemporary American and Canadian literature; periodicals and "middlemen" of letters; and the reception of North American writing in Europe. He has published on Carol Shields, Wayne Johnston and Tomson Highway and is the author of *Malcolm Cowley: The Formative Years* (1993) and editor of *First Nations of North America: Politics and Representation* (2005). He was President of the Association for Canadian Studies in the Netherlands, 2000-2003.

Mark Baker is a translator, editor, and writer based in Utrecht, NL. Born and raised in the UK, he studied German and Drama in London and Berlin before settling in the Netherlands. Moving from legal and commercial translation into the fields of arts and culture, he has worked for most of the major cultural festivals and institutions in the Netherlands. He also translates plays and film scripts, and is the name behind Wordsmiths.

Moritz Baumgaertel was born in Munich, Germany. A graduate of the Roosevelt Academy, Middelburg, NL, he is currently a Master's student in Public International Law at the University of Utrecht, NL. His main research interests are global governance, international public policy networks, and discourse analysis. Moritz hopes to pursue an academic career in the fields of International Law and International Relations.

Pieter Beelaerts van Blokland, Ph.D. President of the national committee, "Thank you Canada & Allied Forces", was a young boy during World War II. Canadian officers were billeted in his family's home. Following a political career in the Dutch government he became Mayor of Apeldoorn in 1981. In 1985, he organized a parade for the 40th anniversary of the liberation, which took place in Apeldoorn and was attended by 3,000 Canadian War Veterans.

Jacqueline Breidlid holds a Bachelor's degree in Social Sciences, with a focus on International Relations and Political Theory, from the Roosevelt Academy, Middelburg, NL, and is currently studying for her Master's degree in Public International Law at the University of Utrecht. Her main interests lie in Human Rights Law, International Environmental Law, and International Relations Theories.

Malcolm Campbell-Verduyn, M.A. is the son of a Dutch-born mother and a Canadian father of French and Scottish background. As part of his Bachelor's degree at York University in Toronto, he participated in an academic exchange at the University of Amsterdam in 2005-2006. After graduating, he returned to the Netherlands to complete his Master's at the University of Leiden in 2008, with a thesis on transatlantic economic relations. He plans to pursue his Ph.D. in the areas of international political economy and global financial governance.

Jesse Coleman, M.A. was born in Calgary, Canada. He majored in Social Psychology and International Relations at the Roosevelt Academy, Middelburg, NL. After receiving his Bachelor's degree he moved to Amsterdam and completed a two-year Research Master's, which included field research in Africa on the use of mobile phones as health care devices (known as "mHealth"). He recently started working for WelTel, an mHealth start-up, in their African division. He hopes to secure a Ph.D. position in the future.

Lia Dell'Orletta and her mother Helena live in Barrie, Ontario, Canada. Named after her Dutch great-aunt who was killed by a bomb in her home in Leidschendam on 27 February 1945 when she was 11 years old, Lia has a deep interest in the contributions and sacrifices of the Canadians on Dutch soil. Together with 2,000 Canadian students and their group leaders, she and her mother, whose parents immigrated to Canada in 1956, travelled to the Netherlands in May 2010 to visit Canadian military cemeteries.

Mary Derr-de Jong is one of 8,000 so-called liberation babies conceived by Allied soldiers with Dutch women. She discovered the identity of her Canadian father only after he had died in 1999. The members of Mary's Canadian family have welcomed her warmly, and she travels regularly to Canada with her husband to visit her four half-sisters and Canadian relatives.

Olga van Ditzhuijzen was born in Alkmaar, NL, in 1976. After completing a law degree in 2002, she decided to follow her childhood dream of becoming a journalist. In 2005, she was accepted in an intensive postgraduate course in newspaper journalism, and since 2006, she has worked as a freelance journalist from her home in Amsterdam. She writes for several newspapers and magazines in the Netherlands, including the Dutch national paper, *NRC Handelsblad*.

Eke Foreman-van der Woude was 19 when she proposed an exchange of eggs for soap to a Canadian soldier named Eldon Foreman who was stationed in her home town of Eelde in May 1945. It was love at first sight. The war bride sailed to Canada to join her new husband, and the couple had many years of happiness together before Eldon died in 2002. At 84, Eke continues to enjoy the Canadian outdoors.

André Gingras was born and educated in Canada, and has made the Netherlands his home since 1998. Trained as a ballet dancer, he performed in New York and Europe before settling in Amsterdam. He appreciates the deep interest that the Dutch have for dance, and is very happy in his new position as director of Dance Works Rotterdam.

Kristen den Hartog is a Canadian novelist and co-author of *The Occupied Garden* (2008) (*De kinderen van de tuinder*). Written with her sister, Tracy Kasaboski, the book explores their grandparents' war experiences near The Hague, and the family's move to Canada in the 1950s. Kristen den Hartog lives and writes in Toronto.

Bob Hofman has been in education all his life. After a career teaching audio visual media at a high school in Uden, he took a position at the International Institute Communication and Development (IICD) in The Hague. He facilitates Learning Circles, a virtual collaboration between high school students around the world on specific themes. In 2005, he initiated the "Echoes" Project, which connects Dutch and Canadian high school students in their search for stories about World War II.

Emma Kutka was born in Toronto and raised in Port Colborne, Ontario, and is now in her third year of an Honours B.A. in Political Studies at Queen's University, Kingston, Ontario. She is currently on a one-year exchange at the University of Groningen, NL. She is interested in how non-Dutch cultures and backgrounds are part of the Dutch identity.

Djeyhoun Ostowar completed an extensive research project on the political and socio-economic position of Russian-speaking minorities in the Baltic States as part of his studies at the Roosevelt Academy, Middelburg, NL. He has represented his university at several international student conferences, and has co-organized seminars, symposia, and lectures in Middelburg, Rotterdam, and The Hague. He has worked for the Refugee Agency and the Red Cross, and is currently Senior Fellow of Humanity in Action, a transatlantic organization for education and the promotion of human and minority rights.

Jan Piëst was a teenager when Groningen was liberated by Canadian troops in April 1945. His appreciation of that day and of the sacrifices made by many Canadian soldiers is expressed in his poem, "The Men of Maple Leaf", which was presented at the 50th anniversary of liberation in 1995 and is on display in Groningen's Martini church as well as at the Canadian embassy in The Hague. Piëst has also written about his war experiences and his meetings with many war veterans in his book, *The True Watcher* (2005).

Hans van Riet, LLM, earned his Bachelor's and Master's degrees in Law and a Minor in English Language and Culture at the University of Utrecht, NL. He added a Minor, "Focus on Canada: An Introduction to Canadian Studies," at Radboud University, Nijmegen, and specialized in International Law. In August 2009, he became legal advisor of the Land Forces of the Royal Dutch Army and attained the rank of Captain. He has travelled widely through Canada.

Sandra van Rijn (neé Vago) is a Canadian citizen born in New York, whose studies, work, and travels have taken her from Montreal to Glasgow, Paris, and St Petersburg, and since 1997, to the city of Leiden, NL, where she lives with her Dutch husband and their daughter, and runs a business selling Canadian maple products. In 2006, she and a friend set up the firm Simply Architects.

Arlinda Rrustemi came to the Roosevelt Academy, Middelburg, NL, from Prishtina, Kosovo. Since graduating, she has enrolled in the Master's program in Public International Law at the University of Utrecht, NL. Her main interests are processes of legal reform and the politics of transition in Kosovo. She has worked as a volunteer in numerous organizations, including the Initiative for Human Rights, the Kosovo Academic Centre, and the Kosovo Youth Network.

Irene Salverda, M.A. was born in 1982 and studied social and cultural anthropology at Radboud University, Nijmegen, NL. Currently, she works as a communications advisor in environmental services. In 2004-2005, Irene lived with the Kwakwaka'wakw First Nations in British Columbia, Canada, to study their treaty processes and traditions. She returns yearly to visit the Kwakwaka'wakw, and writes freelance articles about her travels.

Giles Scott-Smith, Ph.D. is Associate Professor in International Relations at the Roosevelt Academy in Middelburg, NL, and senior researcher with the American Roosevelt Study Center. He also holds the Ernst van der Beugel Chair in Transatlantic Diplomatic History since World War II at Leiden University. His research interests include the role of public diplomacy and private organizations in transatlantic relations since World War II. His most recent book is *Networks of Empire: The US State Department's Foreign Leader Program in the Netherlands, France, and Britain 1950-70* (2008).

Conny Steenman Marcusse, Ph.D. specialized in Canadian and American literature at the University of Leiden, NL, with a focus on the contemporary novel. President of the Association for Canadian Studies in the Netherlands (ACSN) since 2003, she has welcomed many Canadian writers to her home.

Recent publications include two co-editions with Canadian writer Aritha van Herk: *Building Liberty: Canada and World Peace, 1945-2005* (2005) and *Carol Shields: Evocation and Echo* (2009).

Anke Teunissen was born in Drachten, NL, and studied cultural anthropology in Amsterdam before taking up the study of photography at the Royal Academy of Arts in The Hague. Since 2000, she has worked as a freelance and documentary photographer, as well as a film researcher, on commissions such as a series on emigrants, immigrants, and migrants for *Openluchtmuseum* in Arnhem. Her first book of photographs, *Nestblijvers* [Nest clingers], appeared in 2006, on the subject of elderly people living in their parents' homes.

Jeanette den Toonder, Ph.D. is Director of the Centre for Canadian Studies at the University of Groningen, NL, and associate professor of Contemporary French and Francophone literature and culture in the Department of Romance Languages and Cultures. She publishes on the contemporary novel in Quebec, the Acadian novel, and francophone immigrant writing, with a focus on questions of travel, identity, and space. She is co-editor with Jean Morency and Jaap Lintvelt of *Romans de la route et voyages identitaires* (2006), and editor of *Les voix du temps et de l'espace* (2007).

Christl Verduyn, Ph.D. was born in Amsterdam and immigrated with her family to Canada in the 1950s. Professor of Canadian literature and Canadian studies, she has authored, edited, or co-edited a dozen books in these areas. She is a member of the Royal Society of Canada and recipient of the 2006 Governor General's International Award in Canadian Studies. She regularly spends sabbatical time in the Netherlands.

Marijn van Vliet was born and raised in Groningen, NL, and is currently in the final stages of his Bachelor's degree program in International Relations at the University of Groningen, which included a semester at the *Université Laval* in Quebec City in 2009. He plans to pursue his Master's degree and his passion for politics and travel.

Ruben Vroegop, M.A. was born in Maastricht, NL, in 1979, and became a permanent resident of Canada in 2008. A graduate of Radboud University, Nijmegen, NL, he also studied at McGill University and the *Université de Montréal* in Montreal, Canada. He has worked for Dutch, Swiss, and Canadian research institutes, and is currently a defence analyst with the Department of National Defence in Ottawa. An amateur photographer and avid fan of the *Canadien de Montréal*, Ruben lives with the granddaughter of a World War II veteran.